BEYOND POLITICS

BEYOND POLITICS

By
CHRISTOPHER DAWSON

Essay Index Reprint Series

 BOOKS FOR LIBRARIES PRESS
FREEPORT, NEW YORK

First Published 1939
Reprinted 1970

STANDARD BOOK NUMBER:
8369-1603-4

LIBRARY OF CONGRESS CATALOG CARD NUMBER:
74-111825

PRINTED IN THE UNITED STATES OF AMERICA

CONTENTS

I
BEYOND POLITICS

I
BEYOND POLITICS

FOUR years ago I wrote a small book on *Religion and the Modern State* which was an attempt to reconsider the problem of the relations of Church and State as they were affected by the rise of the new political ideologies. I pointed out that the issue was not merely a conflict between Democracy and Dictatorship or between Fascism and Communism. It was a change in the whole social structure of the modern world, which affects religion and culture as well as politics and economics. The forces that make for social uniformity and the mechanization of culture are no less strong in England and the United States than in Germany and Italy, so that we might expect to see the rise of a democratic totalitarianism which would make the same universal claims on the life of the individual as the totalitarian dictatorships of the Continent.

I think that events have justified this diagnosis of the situation and that few people to-day will question the existence of this

3

totalitarian trend even in our own country. It has indeed become the most vital and urgent problem of our time, how this trend is to be reconciled with the traditions of liberty and individualism on which not only the English State but the whole fabric of English culture and social institutions has been built.

Everybody recognizes the need for national unity and national organization, but there are few who realize how fundamental are the changes that this involves in our national ways of life and ways of thought, and fewer still are prepared to pay the price. For if we copy the methods of the dictatorships in a merely negative and defensive spirit, we shall lose our liberty and the distinctive virtues of the English social system without gaining any new inspiration or vision. While if we go the whole way and attempt to base our organization on the positive creed of a political party, we shall run the risk of producing a social conflict which will divide the nation instead of uniting it.

It is easy to take a pessimistic view of the situation and to say that England is now paying the price for the material prosperity and economic domination that she has enjoyed for the last century, and that she must now yield place to the younger and more ruthless powers that have learned in a hard school to adapt themselves to the new conditions. But even if this be true, it is no excuse for an attitude of passive resignation. The change we are witnessing is something much greater than the rise and decline of particular States. It is a transformation of civilization such as the world has never known before, and it affects every nation and every continent, whether they are young or old, whether they are weak or powerful.

What is it that is happening? The old civilization of Western Europe which was so deeply rooted in the Christian and Mediterranean past has produced something different to itself which has no roots in the experience of our race—a marvellous mechanical monster that threatens to devour the culture that created it.

For the most disturbing feature of the new situation is the growing inhumanity of our civilization. It is not that we are personally less humane: on the contrary we are horrified at the cruel sports and cruel punishments of our forefathers in the not remote past. It is the system itself which is indifferent to humanity and which forces its servants and masters to be indifferent also. We see this in detail in the case of the motor-car which exists to serve

human pleasure and convenience and yet inevitably seems to bring mutilation and death
to large numbers of harmless people. We see
it on a large scale in the way that the modern
industrial system, which exists to serve human
needs, nevertheless reduces the countryside to
smoking desolation and involves whole popula-
tions in periodic troughs of depression and
scarcity. But we see it in its most extreme and
devilish form in modern warfare which has a
nightmare quality about it that is hardly
reconcilable with a human origin or purpose.

When we saw the recent preparations for
war—the gas masks, the digging of shelters
and the preparation for the wholesale evacuation
of the population from the towns—it seemed
no longer to have anything in common with
the old warfare of armies set in array and
the human thrill of battle. It was rather as
though a human ant heap was threatened with
destruction by some gigantic impersonal force.

If the world abandons itself to the domination
of these inhuman powers, it matters little which
nation or which group of States is successful,
for this power is alien to every nation, and its
victory means defeat for humanity as a whole.
The militant ideologies of the Left and the Right
may, no doubt, help nations to endure the shock

with fortitude and even with hope, but they are like drugs which render the nerves insensible to the pain of the operation without in any way changing its character. For these gigantic forces seem to demand some superhuman power, some pure intelligence, to govern them, if they are not to become devilish instruments of destruction; and the more completely a nation surrenders itself to the blind urge to power, the more easily are they carried away by the relentless drive of events which is pressing European civilization towards disaster.

The fact is that the same fundamental issues confront all the peoples of Europe, and the Fascist States are no more anxious than the democratic ones to make a complete break with the past. On the contrary, they have taken their stand in the maintenance of national traditions and national culture, and the traditions of Latin and Germanic culture are really no more adapted to mass organization and mechanization than are our own. It is only in the region of politics that their tradition of authoritative government and military discipline have made it easier for them than for ourselves to accept a totalitarian system, but this is not altogether an advantage since it causes the real nature of the change to be obscured by the romance of ideological myths and passionate loyalty to the personality of a leader.

But we have to face these problems in cold blood without any passionate belief in an inspired leader or a new gospel. It is therefore harder for us to take decisions, harder for us to choose a definite path, while on the other hand we still have room to look around and to learn from the mistakes of those who have attempted to solve the problem by drastic revolutionary methods.

Now the existing totalitarian régimes have all originated in the same manner: viz. by the capture of the State machine by a political party which has then proceeded to reorganize the whole life of the community according to its programme and ideology. Under the régime of parliamentary democracy, the State had become a neutral impersonal organization which was operated by whatever party or combination of parties happened to predominate at the moment, and since rival parties and rival interests tended, with universal suffrage and representation, to cancel one another out, the democratic State was incapable of deciding fundamental issues and the whole government became weak and inept.

Fascism and Communism owed their triumph to a policy of revolutionary action which restored to the State a single will and purpose. But in order to do this they narrowed the basis of citizenship at the same time as they widened the range of political action. Alike to the Communist and the National Socialist the Community transcends the State, and the party is not a cog in the machinery of government, but the inspired organ of the Community or the nation and it possesses a divine absolute right to override legal and constitutional restrictions and to use the State as a means of realizing its super-political ideals. For the State exists only to serve the people; and the Party, or the Leader of the Party, is the only authentic embodiment of the will of the people.

Thus the new parties have little in common with their democratic predecessors. They are more like a religious order which exacts total obedience from its members and which trains them by a strict discipline to become the instruments of the corporate purpose. But while a religious order is always in the last resort the servant of the Church, the totalitarian party is the master of the State and bends it to its purpose. It is in fact more like a Church than a State, since its membership is based on the profession of a creed or ideology and on faith in the gospel of the leader rather than on citizenship. Nevertheless, though the Party is above the State and assumes super-political functions, there is an inevitable tendency for it to become fused with it sooner or later.

Alike in Russia, Italy and Germany, it is no longer possible to distinguish the party from the government, so that the upshot of the revolution in all three cases has been an immense increase in the power of the State and in the range of its activities. Never perhaps in the history of the world has the State been so omnipotent and its power so highly concentrated in the hands of the ruler as in the three great totalitarian States to-day. There have been vast empires in the past, and emperors and dictators who seemed to possess unlimited power over their subjects, but never before have they been able to mobilize all the political, economic and psychological resources of the community and turn them to whatever end they chose. De Maistre wrote in a striking phrase of the revolutionary will of the First French Republic as "a battering ram with twenty million men behind it", and this is ten times more true of the will to power of the new totalitarian State, for apart from the greater population and wealth of the new States, their mechanization and their intensive organization of intelligence and propaganda give them a power of which earlier ages had no conception.

Now the problem which confronts us to-day is how the democratic States are to make themselves strong enough to exist in face of the new powers, without abandoning the principles of personal liberty and tolerance on which they are based. And it is a problem on which the future of the world depends, for if the three great western democracies, England, France, and the United States, fail to preserve and maintain their tradition of freedom, no other powers in the world will be strong enough to do so, and the whole spirit of western civilization will be changed.

From the western political standpoint the régime of the totalitarian party State represents a brutal simplification of social life, a one-sided solution which ruthlessly sacrifices some of the highest cultural values to the cult of power. Yet this should not prevent us from recognizing that its achievements are genuine ones or from admitting the weaknesses and vices of our own liberal democratic system and the tendencies towards social degeneration which exist in democratic society.

B

If Western civilization is to be saved it is necessary to find some way of removing the divided aims, the lack of social discipline and the absence of national unity that are the weaknesses of democracy, without falling under the *tyrannis* of dictatorship and the fanatical intolerance of a totalitarian party. And we cannot do this by politics alone. No constitutional change will touch the roots of our weakness, for it is the life of society and not merely the government of society that needs reordering. It is through their realization of that truth that the dictators have earned their success. They have not been content to govern and tax and legislate, they have aspired to change the spirit of a people, to rescue it from apathy and despair, to give it faith in its mission and hope in its future. And if they have done it by crude and brutal methods, by the sacrifice of individual freedom and by the suppression and oppression of minorities, they would say that it is better to do it so than not to do it at all.

But we on our side must ask whether it is not possible for a free nation to do all this without losing its freedom and by methods which do not conflict with the social traditions of our race. After all, Communism had behind it the tradition of autocratic violence which had already revolutionized the Russian State in the days of Peter the Great, while National Socialism can appeal to the tradition of a State that was built up by military discipline and the ideal of a people in arms.

We, on the other hand, have behind us a yet longer tradition of freedom; not, it is true, of democracy in the modern sense, but of individual liberty and corporate self-government. Our parliamentary institutions are not the artificial creation of liberal idealism, as in so many countries; they are an organic part of the life of the nation, and they have grown up century by century by the vital urge of social realities. We are too old to change this tradition for some imported ideology. If parliamentary institutions are unreconcilable with a totalitarian party régime (and I believe they are) then the new system is not for us. We must find some other method of reorganizing and strengthening the nation.

The British parliamentary system is of its very nature non-totalitarian, and its success through the ages has been largely due to the limited character of its aims and its powers. It has been the monarchy rather than parliament that has been the symbol and guarantee of national unity, and the monarchy, even more than parliament, depends for its very existence on its limited character. But what has always given the English system its unique strength and social solidity has been the existence of a social unity behind the monarchy and behind parliament, a unity of which they are the political organs, but which itself transcends politics. It is this unity which makes it possible for our party system to function on a basis of common understanding without dividing the nation into two hostile camps with mutually exclusive ideologies.

In the past this unity was taken for granted: it was an unconscious social fact arising out of the natural structure of society, from the life of the people and the national tradition of culture. But to-day not only is this structure changing, it is also becoming self-conscious owing to the advance in psychological knowledge and the organization of sociological and economic research. And it is on this ground, rather than in the field of politics in the strict sense, that it is necessary to plan and organize, if any fundamental reform is to be made in the life of the nation.

It is true that the totalitarian States have attempted this fundamental work of social

reconstruction by direct political action. But
by so doing they have, as we have seen, made
the party into a super-political organization
which has some of the characteristics of a
religious society, and at the same time they
have destroyed personal freedom and narrowed
the national tradition of culture by sub-
ordinating the higher super-political activities
of the community to the intolerant and rigid
tyranny of political partisanship.

In the past Western society was made up
of a number of interpenetrating orders, political,
economic, cultural and religious, each of which
was either autonomous or possessed a considerable degree of *de facto* independence. The
political order was only a part, and in theory
at least not the most important part, of the
social structure, and within the political order
itself the party held a relatively humble and
unhonoured place. The idea that the spiritual
life of society should be ruled and guided by a
political party would have appeared to our
ancestors a monstrous absurdity. The spiritual
order possessed its own organization, that of
the Church, which was held to transcend all
the rest in importance and which exercised a
profound influence on human life from the
cradle to the grave.

But the time has long passed since the Church held undisputed sway over the mind and conscience of western culture, and the loss of Christian unity has brought with it a loss of spiritual order and of the sense of spiritual values in society at large. First, with the Renaissance, secular culture emancipated itself from the tutelage of the Church and created an independent order of humanism and science. Then with the industrial revolution economic life emancipated itself from the control of the State and created the vast system of financial, commercial and industrial relations which we know as the capitalist order.

Thus there have arisen outside the traditional historic organizations of Church and State these two independent orders to which western civilisation owes a vast increase in its material and spiritual resources, but which on account of this lack of organization and social direction, have become centrifugal and disintegrating forces. This first became plainly evident in regard to economics, and it was here that the first conscious attempt was made to restore unity of direction and bring the economic order under the control of the community. This was the origin of Socialism and, in a sense, of all the totalitarian movements, for the

attempt to unify the political and the economic
orders led almost inevitably to the confusion
of social categories and the attempt to extend
State control to every sphere of social life.
Even in England, I believe that the decline of
our political system dates from the day when
the Trade Unions renounced their non-political
ideal of being masters in their own house and
aspired to be masters also in the House of
Commons. For this led inevitably to the
supersession of the Liberal Party, which was a
vital organ of English political life, and the
intrusion of a new principle which if logically
carried out would involve a totalitarian order.
For if all the workers are embodied in the
unions, and if the T.U.C. decides the policy of
its parliamentary candidates, it is obvious
that the English party system could no longer
exist, and the whole political order would be
subordinated to an organization based on
industry and governed by purely economic
considerations.

Actually, of course, these possibilities have
failed to materialize and the Labour Party,
instead of absorbing the political in the economic
order, has helped to bring some measure of social
responsibility and control into the capitalist
system. Nevertheless, the creation of a party

that has a non-political economic basis and the introduction of the principle of class war into the party system have undoubtedly weakened and narrowed the basis of agreement on which that system rests, and there can be little doubt that an attempt to realize the full socialist programme by constitutional means would strain the parliamentary system to breaking point.

But if it is dangerous to attempt the fundamental reorganization of economic life by purely political means, it is far more dangerous to bring politics into the order of culture, for this means the invasion of the human soul by the hand of power. This is the original sin of every totalitarian system, and this is why the English mind revolts instinctively at the idea of the forcible imposition by the State of any kind of ideology.

When Humanism emancipated secular culture from ecclesiastical control, it applied the traditional mediæval ideal of the freedom of the spiritual power to the realm of science and art. It sought not the destruction of the spiritual power, but the creation of an independent spiritual power in the natural order; and ever since then the freedom of scholarship and science and art has been the keystone of western culture.

But the republic of letters was never a lawless one. Citizenship could only be obtained by a long and toilsome discipline which made the scholars no less a closed and privileged order than the clerics of the mediæval Church.

But modern civilization, while retaining the ideal of freedom of thought, and even extending it to regions which were formerly outside its domain, has at the same time destroyed the framework of social and intellectual discipline on which this freedom rested. With the growth of popular education at one end of the scale, and the development of scientific specialization at the other, the intellectual order dissolved into a vast and formless chaos controlled only by the power of the state over education and the power of capital over the press. Where these powers do not operate, the strange shadow world of the intelligentsia remains the last refuge of cultural independence like the last spot of dry land on which man and beast crowd together in uneasy fellowship before the rising floods.

Unless some order can be brought back into this chaos, nothing can save it from the ideological police of a totalitarian State, and there is already no lack of evidence of what that involves in the loss of spiritual freedom and the lowering of cultural standards. Better perhaps that the State should organize our culture than that it should be left to the mercenary leadership of the popular press and the financial exploitation of its intellectual and moral weakness. But it is a choice of evils, either of which is equally hostile to the freedom and humanity of western culture.

But what of the other spiritual power which still survives and still maintains its ancient claim to be the guide and teacher of mankind—I mean the Church? There is no doubt that the Church is by its nature and tradition better fitted to deal with problems of the spiritual order than the State can ever be. "Let us not forget," wrote Nietzsche, "in the end what a Church is and especially in contrast to every 'State', a Church is above all an authoritative organization which secures to the most *spiritual* men the highest rank, and *believes* in the power of spirituality so far as to forbid all grosser appliances of authority. Through this alone the Church is under all circumstances a *nobler* institution than the State."

Nevertheless it is to-day impossible to return to the undifferentiated unity of mediæval culture. The rise of humanism and the modern sciences has created an autonomous sphere of culture

which lies entirely outside the ecclesiastical
domain and in which any direct intervention
on the part of the Church would be resented
as an intrusion. Moreover, the Church is herself
weakened by religious division and invaded
on her own territory by the forces of anti-
clericalism and paganism, and by the unlimited
claims of the totalitarian State.

The greatest service the Church can render
to western civilization at the present time is
to keep her own inheritance intact and not to
allow her witness to be obscured by letting
herself be used as the instrument of secular
powers and politics.

It is true that the present crisis is producing
constant appeals to the Church to use her
influence in the cause of "moral rearmament".
There is a tendency, especially among the
English-speaking Protestant peoples, to treat
religion as a kind of social tonic that can be
used in times of national emergency in order
to extract a further degree of moral effort from
the people. But apart from the Pelagian conception of religion that this view implies, it
is not wholly sound from the psychological
point of view, since it merely heightens the
amount of moral tension without increasing
the sources of spiritual vitality or resolving the

psychological conflicts from which the society suffers.

Moreover, moral rearmament to serve the cause of the nation is not the Church's primary and essential task. Religion serves a higher creed than man can comprehend. Again and again we see the prophets, and One greater than the prophets, announcing the doom of their people, when on the short view they should have been devoting their energies to restoring the national morale. Certainly no modern government, whether totalitarian or democratic, would tolerate the behaviour of Jeremiah the prophet at the time of his nation's need: in fact in most countries to-day his treatment would be condemned as unduly mild, and he would be executed out of hand as an agent of enemy propaganda.

Yet on the long view Jeremiah is justified even on national grounds, since, thanks to him and his like, his people still survive while the successful powers to which they bowed their neck have one after another gone down to the dust. Better for Israel, some may say, if they had shared the lot of other peoples and not continued to drag their weary way down twenty-five centuries of suffering. But that is where history, like religion, transcends the order

of culture and enters the penumbra of divine
mystery.

And the Church, no less than the ancient
prophets, is the servant of this higher order.
She is the hierophant of the divine mysteries,
not the teacher of human science nor the
organizer of human culture. But if it is not the
Church's business to organize culture, neither
is it that of the State. It is an intermediate
region which belongs to neither the one nor the
other, but which has its own laws of life and its
own right to self-determination and self-
direction.

To restore order in this sphere is the greatest
need of our civilization, but it can only be
achieved by a power of its own order, that is
to say by the power of ideas and the organization
of thought. But it is not possible to do this
by any kind of philosophic or scientific dictatorship, as was the dream of the idealists from
Plato to the present day, for the intellectual
world is as divided as the religious world, and
philosophy has lost its ancient prestige and its
hegemony over the other sciences.

Nor is it possible to restore spiritual order
by a return to the old humanist discipline of
letters, for that is inseparable from the aristocratic ideal of a privileged caste of scholars.

A democratic society must find a correspondingly democratic organization of culture, which should be distinct from political democracy, but parallel to it in another field of activity. At the present day, when everyone is educated a little, and when no one can master the whole realm of knowledge, it would be invidious to distinguish the scholars from the unlearned, especially since under modern conditions a man may attain vast scientific knowledge without any corresponding breadth of culture.

In these circumstances it seems to me that the form of organization appropriate to our society in the field of culture as well as in that of politics is the party—that is to say a voluntary organization for common ends based on a common "ideology".

But is an organization of this kind conceivable in our divided and disordered civilization? That is the vital question on which the future of democracy depends.

The totalitarian parties, as I have pointed out, owe their success to their achievement in this field—the organization of national life and culture outside the political sphere. But since this function is not really consistent with the political basis of their activity, they tran-

scend politics in both directions—by aiming at
a super-political end and by using sub-political
methods of violence and lawlessness in order
to attain it. They become persecuting sects,
like the Jacobins before them, rather than free
organs of public opinion.

Now it is the fundamental principle of the
old English school of political thought that the
national society and national culture transcend
politics. It is common both to the Left and the
Right, and was insisted on by Tom Paine as
strongly as by Edmund Burke. Government,
says the former, is no sacred mystery, it is
simply a national association for carrying on
the public business—*res publica*—and the greater
part of the order that reigns among mankind
is not the creation of governments, but is due
to the free activity of the civilized community.
Society, says Burke, is not an artificial legal
construction, it is a spiritual community, "a
partnership in all science, a partnership in all
art, a partnership in every virtue and in all
perfection. As the ends of such a partnership
cannot be obtained in many generations, it
becomes a partnership not only between those
who are living, but between those who are
living, those who are dead and those who are
yet to be born."

But while English thinkers, whether Liberal or Conservative, recognized that society transcends the State, they did not realize the need for any deliberate organization of the non-political social functions. They believed that these things could be safely left to nature and to the free activity of individuals or, alternatively, to nature and social tradition. They did not see that some form of social control is necessary in the economic world in order to protect the individual and society itself from exploitation, and that some social discipline is no less necessary in the world of culture to save the national tradition from disintegration and destruction.

To-day the liberal individualism and the conservative traditionalism of the nineteenth century have alike disappeared, and the policy of *laissez faire*, which has already been abandoned in economics, is rightly being abandoned in culture also. Nevertheless, this need not involve the abandonment of the traditional English principle of the limitation of the State to its own political sphere. It is still possible to create an organization of national culture which would not be directly dependent on the State or on any political party; and I believe that a society so organized would be not only more free but in the last resort also stronger than a totalitarian State which is obliged to narrow and even impoverish its culture in order to keep it completely dependent on political control.

But in order to do this it is necessary to have a clear consciousness of our aim, and to pursue it with as much determination and perseverence as the servants of the State have shown in their domain. Hitherto the children of this world have shown themselves not only wiser but also more capable of self-discipline and devotion than the children of light. The Machiavellian virtue of the statesman, low as it may be, has been a real thing, whereas the higher ideals of the humanist and the philosopher have been bloodless phantoms which were not strong enough to arouse passionate devotion or effectual action.

Yet few would deny that it is possible to serve the community in other fields than politics, or would hold that such a vocation is intrinsically less capable of arousing devotion and enthusiasm. What has been lacking hitherto is any satisfactory basis for common action, and for lack of this there has been an appalling waste and misdirection of the highest spiritual resources of the community which have been

c

left to run wild or to expend themselves in an unworthy servitude to economic interests.

What is necessary is some organization which is neither political nor economic, and which will devote itself to the service of national life and the organization of national culture. At the present time in democratic countries the realm of culture has become a no-man's-land which is given up to anarchic individualism and at the same time invaded from different directions by the organized powers of the State, and financial capitalism. Thus the press, the cinema, and the theatre, which exert such an enormous influence on public opinion and popular culture, are as yet almost free in democratic countries from any direct interference by the State: yet their freedom is limited and their cultural value diminished in every direction by the financial motives and the capitalist organization that determine their character. The field of education, on the other hand, is relatively free from this slavery to economic forces. But here the State has already acquired almost complete control, and it would seem as though the power which the State has thus obtained over the mind of the community must inevitably bring about the triumph of a totalitarian order.

Nevertheless, there remains a free element, a

survival of the humanist tradition, which gives even our bureaucratic educational machine a leaven of freedom and liberal ideals. It is easy to condemn the snobbery and Philistinism of the English public-school system. Yet one must admit, I think, that it does stand, however incompletely, for this principle of the service of the national culture, apart from any political or economic motive; so that one is conscious of the presence of something which comes neither from State organization nor the power of money, but which is the fruit of the unbroken corporate tradition of centuries of national life. It is inevitable that under existing social conditions some of them should have acquired a definitely aristocratic character as the preserve of a wealthy and privileged class, but this is by no means always the case. The school which I know best, and which is in a sense the archetype of the whole system, has never had any marked aristocratic or plutocratic character. It has always maintained its original function of training scholars who would be good servants of the community. In this it has been faithful to the spirit of its founder, the good chancellor, who was the trusty servant alike of King and Pope, of State and Church, of England and Christendom.

And thus it has preserved its place through all the social and political changes of five centuries as an independent spiritual organ of the community, a living example of an organized cultural institution which is neither the creature of the State nor the servant of the financial powers that dominate democratic society.

Now if it is possible for a school to have an independent cultural tradition and, as it were, a soul of its own, why should not the same principle of free organization be applied to other fields of culture which at present lie derelict and which otherwise will become the drill fields and machine yards of a totalitarian State?

The main cause is the absence of any spiritual power to take the work in hand and the lack of any clear sense of national aims and social responsibility in matters of culture. But the time has come when we can no longer afford to neglect the non-political and non-economic sides of national life or to leave them to the unorganized activity of individuals. The new totalitarian parties and régimes have discovered that nations do not live by bread alone and they have attempted to capture the soul of a nation by violence and to use the total psychological force of the community in their relentless drive towards world power. Thus what is at stake is not the literary culture of a privileged minority, but the spiritual life of the people. It is only by the free organization of national life, according to the spirit of our institutions and traditions, but in new forms adapted to twentieth-century conditions, that we can save, not only our national being, but also the ways of life, the forms of thought and the spiritual values which are the principles of Western Civilization.

II
POLITICS AND NATIONAL CULTURE

II

POLITICS AND NATIONAL CULTURE

THE growing complication of modern mechanized civilization, especially in the more highly industrialized countries, demands a correspondingly higher degree of organization. This organization cannot be limited to the material elements in the complex, it extends inevitably to society itself and through society to the ethical and psychological life of the individual. Hence the historical trend has been from politics to sociology. Problems which were a century ago regarded as purely political, became economic in the second half of the nineteenth century and during the present century have become sociological and psychological ones. But public opinion as yet is not fully aware of this change. Society is adapting itself as it were unconsciously and instinctively to the new conditions, and much of the tension and unrest of the present time is due to the inadequacy of our inherited stock of social traditions to cope with the realities of the situation, and the difficulty of squaring the already emergent

35

system of social organization with political theories and social doctrines to which we still consciously adhere, but which are to a great extent irrelevant to the modern situation.

Nevertheless, attempts have already been made, under the pressure of political and economic necessity, to construct new forms of government and corresponding systems of ideas which will provide a basis for the necessary process of social reorganization. These are the so-called "totalitarian" régimes and ideologies which attempt to make a clean sweep of the débris of nineteenth century institutions and ideas and to build a unitary social structure on new foundations. But owing to the circumstances of their origin—to the unpreparedness of public opinion and the lack of any solid foundation of sociological and psychological knowledge—it was inevitable that these attempts should have involved a drastic simplification of the problems, so that they have swept aside or "liquidated" every social and ideological element which could not be brought into immediate harmony with the dominant party and its creed.

The tragedy is that this simplification is progressive and cumulative. The one-sidedness of Communism in Russia provoked by reaction the opposed one-sidedness of Fascism, which in turn encourages democratic opinion to formulate itself with a new exclusiveness against the dictatorships. If this tendency were carried to its logical conclusion, it would result in the creation of a "democratic" totalitarianism which might be no less narrow and tyrannical than either Communism or National Socialism. Yet on the other hand the need for a higher degree of social organization and a deeper sense of community is one that cannot be ignored and no solution is to be found in a negative resistance to totalitarianism which would attempt to anchor itself to the political ideas of a vanishing state of society.

We need social reorganization no less than the countries of eastern and central Europe. But we cannot achieve it by the simple and drastic methods of revolutionary dictatorship. The countries that have adopted this solution have an authoritarian tradition in government and society. In Russia the new régime arose immediately out of the ruins of the Tsarist autocracy. In Germany it had behind it the Prussian tradition of military discipline and the Bismarckian ideal of an authoritarian State socialism, while in Italy and Spain Fascism represents a reaction from a somewhat exotic and unassimilated Liberalism towards the native Latin tradition of authority and order.

In the West, however, and especially in England, parliamentary government and the party system are not modern innovations that have been introduced from abroad and adapted more or less to a social structure that was built on different foundations. They are part of our historical tradition and have arisen out of the social experience of centuries. In contrast to Russia, where the opposition was a revolutionary movement that was treated by the government as a criminal conspiracy, the English Opposition has always been a vital organ of English political society. So that the modern tendency to import the exclusivism of continental Left —Right ideologies into the English party system, not only falsifies its natural genius, but destroys the very basis of English political life.

The English parties were never the organs of conscious exclusive political ideologies bent on destroying one another and remoulding the State according to a rigid preconceived pattern. They were fluid and variable organizations which represented in a haphazard and unsystematic fashion the dominant social and economic interests in English society and adapted themselves to the changing circumstances of the political situation.

Thus whatever generalization we may make concerning the English parties invariably fails to cover the illogical realities of the situation. For instance we may legitimately speak of the eighteenth century Tories as representing the landed interest and the Whigs the commercial, but we must remember at the same time that the Whigs were the party of the great landlords and that the strongest Tories were to be found among townsmen like Dr. Johnson.

In the same way, in the nineteenth century it is natural to regard the Liberals as the progressive party—the party of reform, and the Conservatives as the representatives of tradition. Yet the traditionalism of English political life is far better represented by the Liberal leaders, Gray, Palmerston, Gladstone, Harcourt, than by the brilliant and exotic individualism of Disraeli, the creator of modern Conservatism; while even in the field of social and humanitarian reform it was Tories like Wilberforce and Shaftesbury who respectively led the struggle against the slave trade, and against the exploitation of women and children in the mines and factories.

The English parties did not, save at rare moments, stand for any coherent body of ideas. They were more like two sides in a political game in which the players were recruited from a limited number of ruling families and were backed by all kinds of local, economic and personal interests. The game was the thing, and political programmes and principles were valid only in so far and so long as they helped the game. In fact it is characteristic of English political life that the ideologists and the political idealists have always tended to become off-side. They have either been sent off the political field, like the Nonjurors or Bolingbroke, or they have changed sides, like Burke and Gladstone.

Yet the English party system worked not only in spite of, but apparently because of its incoherence and illogicality. Whereas a party system which bases itself on clearly defined ideological oppositions, as in France during the Revolution, or on the continent in the Post-War period has led almost infallibly to mutual proscriptions and the liquidation of minorities, until no solution remained save that of dictatorship.

The truth is, unpalatable though it may be to modern "progressive" thought, that democracy and dictatorship are not opposites or mortal enemies, but twin children of the great Revolution, and that the English political system is immune from the tendency towards dictatorship because it is not democratic in the full sense of the word, but rather liberal and aristocratic. The English tradition attaches far more importance to freedom and toleration than does the continental; it developed in defence of individual liberty (and also class privilege) against the State. Continental democracy, on the other hand, was essentially the affirmation of the supremacy of the General Will as against class privilege. It attached more importance to equality and to freedom and to the sovereignty of the people than to the toleration of minorities.

Consequently when we talk of democracy as the common cause of the western peoples against dictatorship, we are using the word in an equivocal sense to cover two distinct systems and traditions, which are indeed in alliance for the time being, but are very far from being identical. For the European political tradition (leaving Russia out of account) is threefold and not twofold, and much of the confusion and incoherence of modern political discussion is due to our failure to recognize this simple fact.

English Parliamentarism is no less different from French Democracy than it is from German Nationalism, though the political circumstances of the moment have drawn us closer to the one and further from the other, just as, at the beginning of the nineteenth century, they had the reverse effect, bringing us closer to Germany and alienating us from France.

The existence of this ideological trinity has indeed always been obscured by the tendency of international policy to divide Europe into two camps, whether by the conscious attempt to realize a balance of power, or by the spontaneous resistance of the majority of States to the domination of a single power (the Spain of Philip II, the France of Louis XIV and of Napoleon or the Germany of William II and of Hitler). It is natural enough that such an opposition should seek an ideological basis and tend to transform itself into a war of ideas—of Catholicism against Protestantism, of the Revolution against Monarchy, or of Democracy against Dictatorship. Nevertheless the common front is seldom a united one, and as in the past Catholic France allied herself with Moslem Turkey and Protestant Sweden against the other Catholic powers—Austria and Spain, so to-day western democracy allies itself with the dictatorship of Moscow against those of Berlin and Rome.

But when we come to the problem of internal social organization, it is necessary to disregard these sham façades of international unity and to go down to the bed rock of our own native tradition. It is no use reorganizing our national life according to the abstract principles of international democracy, for that would lead us to ignore the portion of our social inheritance which is most distinctive of our tradition and which is the root of our national liberties.

Our problem is not to create a totalitarian democratic system, any more than a Communist or a Fascist State. It is to reinterpret the English ideals of freedom and toleration in accordance with the requirements of a post-individualist and post-capitalist age. There is no denying the difficulty of the task, for the whole tendency of modern scientific mass organization, whether democratic or authoritarian, seems opposed to the principles of individual liberty and personal responsibility which are the very soul of English institutions. By the time John Bull has been drilled and rationalized and psycho-analysed, there will be no John Bull left, and yet the old original obstinate and honest English yeoman is an obvious anachronism, whereas German

D

Michael can live on in a brown shirt just as well as he did in the uniform of the Pomeranian Grenadiers.

If the English tradition and English political and social ideals are to survive we have got to find a *via media* between the totalitarian socialism of the dictatorships which is alien to our culture and the liberal individualism which was consonant with our traditions but which belongs to the past —to *our* past, but still the past.

For although liberal individualism may be fossilized or extinct, the ideals behind it which gave it whatever spiritual value it possessed, the ideals of liberty and toleration, are by no means dead, even though they seem threatened with extinction, and any attempt to achieve a social organization adapted to our national genius must hold these ideals in view.

I do not of course intend to suggest that we should take Liberalism in the traditional party sense as our national ideology and organize on that basis. If this be Liberalism it is a Liberalism which transcends political parties. For it is essential that our national ideology should find room for both the great political traditions that have contributed in almost equal measure to our historical development, and as our political ideal has been not the elimination of minority opinion but the co-operation of opposing parties in the service of the nation, so our national ideology must in some way or other reconcile the diverse and apparently contradictory streams of national tradition in the unity of the national culture.

This is a difficult task but it is by no means an impossible one, since our culture already comprehends these traditions, as our polity includes the parties. What is necessary is to transform this unconscious sociological comprehension into a conscious ideological one. In fact it should be easier to-day than it was in the nineteenth century, since the nation has become far more unified from the sociological point of view than it was a hundred years ago. In the nineteenth century there were indeed two Englands— the England of the fields and the England of the factories—and at the time of the Chartist movement it seemed as though this social dualism would find open expression in a revolutionary movement that would have split England asunder. Actually, however, the conflict found a thoroughly bourgeois solution in the struggle for Free Trade, and the incipient class war of the 'thirties and 'forties, which made so deep an impression on Engels and Marx, disappeared before the success of the Victorian compromise.

To-day, on the other hand, when class consciousness and the ideology of social revolution have reached a far higher pitch of development, English society itself has become far more uniform owing to the spread of the new mechanized and standardized culture and the development of the social services. There is no longer the same difference between town and country or between class and class as there was even a generation ago. The wireless and the cinema, motor transport, the popular press and public education have broken down class distinctions and regional differences, and are rapidly creating social uniformity, so that the whole of England from the housing-estate to the luxury flat is inhabited by one gigantic middle class, whose members are only differentiated by graduations of income.

At first sight it may seem that this development will of itself produce the new forms of social organization which the present age requires, and all that is necessary is to bring it into accord with our political tradition of parliamentary government. This is, in fact, what many people understand by modern democracy, and if it were true, it would suffice to account for the reaction against democracy that we see going on in the world at the present time. For if democracy means nothing more than the destruction of social inequality and the reduction of our culture to the lowest common factor of intelligence, then the resultant mass society can be governed more simply and efficiently by a unified dictatorial system than by the relatively complicated and diffuse methods of representative parliamentary government.

In reality, the existing tendency towards social uniformity is far from solving the problem of social organization; it merely provides the material, the unorganized mass, which has to be informed by a living spirit and ordered to some higher end. Without this, social uniformity can mean no more than a reversion to tribal barbarism, and democracy nothing more than the rule of the herd.

Obviously there is no room in such a society for liberty, as it has been understood in the past. For liberty is not the right of the mass to power, but the right of the individual and the group to achieve the highest possible degree of self-development. Hence liberty has always been an aristocratic ideal and it is no accident that England, the home of parliamentary

institutions and political liberties, should also
have been the European State which possessed
the strongest and most unbroken tradition of
aristocratic government.

It is the survival of the vestiges of this
aristocratic tradition which, in spite of the
progress of democracy and social uniformity,
renders English society so recalcitrant to
totalitarian ideas. A pure democracy which
sets equality above every other social value
can adapt itself to a totalitarian organization
as easily as a pure autocracy; but a totalitarian
aristocracy has never existed, and though the
English State may well lose what remains of its
aristocratic institutions, it cannot divest itself
of the values and ideals that were developed by
this political tradition without a loss of national
character, in other words without losing its
own soul.

The English State in the past has been the
classical example of that mixed constitution
which was the political ideal of St. Thomas
Aquinas. And just as it succeeded in developing
self-government without abandoning the historic
tradition of monarchy, so too English democracy
must preserve the vital elements of the aristocratic tradition in so far as they can be adapted
and reinterpreted according to the needs of

our time. Above all the principles of personal honour and individual responsibility, which have always been the life blood of freedom in the ancient world and in medieval and modern Europe alike, must be preserved at all costs, if democracy is to be a community of free men and not an inhuman anonymous servile State.

It is the loss of these principles which is to the English mind the greatest evil of the new totalitarian régimes—an evil which far exceeds the loss of purely political rights. We see this evil in its most shocking form in the horrible self-surrender of the accused in the Russian State trials, but it is endemic in the whole system of propaganda and mass suggestion, spying and delation, persecution and terrorism which forms the dark and sinister underside of the new totalitarian régimes.

But it is not enough for us to repudiate these evils in principle and to congratulate ourselves on the moral superiority of western democracy. For democracy, as I have pointed out, is no safeguard against such things: indeed in so far as democracy involves the standardization and mechanization of culture and the supremacy of the mass over the individual, it is a positive danger. It is inevitable that the disappearance

of a privileged class and the advent of social
uniformity should tend to reduce the value of
the individual and to make the State and other
forms of organization more ready to take
advantage of his defencelessness, unless a
deliberate attempt is made to find some sub-
stitute for the old aristocratic and bourgeois
safeguards of personal liberty.

The essential condition of an order that
corresponds with the spirit of our institutions
and our national tradition is that it should be
a community of free men, and if that is
secured, it is of very secondary importance
whether our political ideology is nominally
democratic or liberal or socialist or nationalist.
In order to survive under the new conditions
a State must possess a higher measure of social
unity, and a more complete integration of the
different forces in the national life than in the
past. And our especial task is to do this
without sacrificing quality to quantity or freedom to mechanical efficiency.

Hence, in the first place, we cannot base our
organization on the totalitarian ideologies of
continental Europe, whether communist or
fascist, for these run counter to our national
political traditions and sacrifice freedom to
organization without any scruple. They repre-

sent, in fact, as I have said, although in very different forms, the adaptation of the political tradition of absolutism and authoritarianism to the conditions of a new age.

In the second place we cannot base our organization on the ideology of a political party. Any national organization must transcend party divisions, for the co-existence of political parties within the political structure is one of the characteristic features of the English system. Hence it is probable that the political parties will tend to become less important, without ceasing to exist as part of the machinery of government, a development which has already made considerable progress during the last quarter of the century.

There remains a third alternative which is much more in accordance with English traditions, but which none the less does not seem to be capable of meeting our present need. It is to co-ordinate and direct public policy and social activities by the private initiative of influential persons or groups of persons, so that the nation is unconsciously guided by its social leaders toward the ends which the latter have determined.

The success of the English system in the past has been largely due to the way in which the public working of our political and legal institutions has been supplemented by this private collaboration between the ruling elements in society. It is to be seen at its best in times of national emergency, when all the resources of social influence are mobilized in the national interest, and it is to be seen in a lower form in the private intrigues and wire pulling that are so often the power behind the scenes in politics and finance. It is this social background of English politics which has been satirized with bitterness and exaggeration, but not without a considerable element of truth, in Mr. Belloc's political novels. But it is for the most part an unknown country to the historian and the political theorist who confine their attention to the foreground of politics and diplomacy.

Now this system of private collaboration and social influence seems to provide the obvious English solution of the problem of social organization. And in fact of late years we have seen considerable attempts being made to utilise these forces for social organization and reform. We see it in such movements as Boy Scouts which is older and in some respects more effective than the elaborate State-controlled youth movements of the Communists and the Fascists. We see it in a more highly

organized form in the manifold development of
voluntary organizations which have grown up
since the War to cover almost every side of
social activity.

This voluntary, though not altogether spontaneous process of socializing national life
through non-political channels without any
definite ideology and with a complete absence
of any revolutionary aim, goes some way toward
satisfying the need for a higher measure of
social integration.   But if it has no strong
emotional impulse behind it, and no clear
consciousness of its final ends, a movement of
this kind tends to become soft and flaccid
and loses itself in a maze of committees and
petty activities. The aristocratic principle of
leadership is most effective at short range and
among a limited circle. When it is diffused
throughout a uniform middle-class society, it
loses in character and quality what it gains in
range and breadth of influence. For example
the public school spirit obviously meant more
when there were half a dozen public schools
than it does to-day when there are a hundred.
And when the ruling class had a definite
economic basis in landownership it had more
cohesion and more social unity than to-day when
it is based on the fluid unstable foundations of

the Stock Exchange and the state of the world markets.

A real social organization of the nation needs something stronger behind it than the social influence of the economically successful classes and a vague general ideal of social service. These by themselves are incapable of resisting the formidable pressure that is exerted by the organized international mass movements of the Left and the Right. If the English tradition is to survive it is necessary to renounce all thought of a Common Front and to stand on our own ground. We need a definite organization which does not compete with that of the political parties, but which is strong enough and conscious enough to meet the competitive organizations and ideologies of Communism and Fascism.

Now the new totalitarian parties differ from the old parliamentary ones not only by their exclusiveness and their use of violent methods. They also cover a much wider field of social activity and attempt to deal with deeper and more fundamental issues. They are in fact cultural as well as political organizations and it is in this field that their most striking successes have been won.

Clearly our parliamentary parties cannot

hope to rival the totalitarian parties in this direction. For they are essentially limited organizations which cannot claim to be the exclusive organs of the nation's life, and our political liberties and our personal freedom depend on these limitations being preserved. But the fact that our political parties are not in a position to assume the wider cultural functions of the totalitarian parties should not cause us to underestimate the importance of these functions. We need something of the nature of a non-political party of national culture to cover the ground that is left un-occupied—the issues outside party politics which are nevertheless essential to the national life. Such an organization would have to be completely free and non-official, since its supreme end must be to preserve the freedom of our national culture. It must find room for everyone who is not committed to a totalitarian ideology and who is loyal to the national tradition and to national institutions and ideals.

There are obvious difficulties in the way of creating such an organization. Nevertheless there have been parties of ideas in the past, for instance, the Action Française and the Fabian Society, and though these aspired to direct political action in the last resort, I do not see

why this should be the inevitable condition of
their existence.

Up to now the cultural and super political
aspects of national life have been taken for
granted and left to the unorganized action of
individuals. It is true that in practice the
advance of national education and the social
services has already brought a whole complex
of cultural activities and problems within
the competence of the State. But "the
State" in this sense means the hierarchy
of the civil servants and the bureaucracy,
rather than the party politicians, and the
cultural ideals of the former were derived
from the traditions of the universities rather
than from the ideology of any particular political
party. And beyond the range of State intervention, a whole world of private intellectual
interests and social activities remained un-
touched and unorganized.

But the coming of the totalitarian régimes
has put an end to this rule of *laissez faire* in
national culture. They have shown that a
nation that organizes the whole of its social
life gains an immense access of strength, even
though we may consider that the price paid for
it is too high. It is even questionable whether
a nation that remains unorganized will be able

to survive the shock of the gigantic forces that are moving in the world to-day. If therefore we wish to maintain our existence without sacrificing our freedom, we must organize as completely as the totalitarian States have done, but in a different way. That is to say we cannot make the political party or the bureaucratic system the sole basis of organization. We must create a new institution or new institutions for the organization of national culture and these institutions must be no less free than our traditional political institutions. Only in this way, it seems to me, will it be possible for us to escape the two opposing dangers that threaten the modern community; on the one hand, the intolerance and loss of personal freedom which are involved in the dictatorship of a political party, and on the other, the degeneration of our culture into a mechanized mass civilization which is as hostile to personal freedom and to intellectual integrity as any form of dictatorship.

III

THE TOTALITARIAN STATE AND THE CHRISTIAN COMMUNITY

III

THE TOTALITARIAN STATE AND THE CHRISTIAN COMMUNITY

A FRUITFUL consideration of the problems of the Christian community is only possible if it is grounded on a full awareness of our own social situation, for that situation not only inevitably determines our historical perspective but also conditions our conceptions of the spiritual problem itself. It is obvious that the spiritual problem of St. Augustine was very different from that of St. Paul, as that of Innocent III was different from that of Leo XIII or that of St. Francis from that of St. Ignatius. And we must remember that the ordinary man is far more deeply involved in the limitations of time and place than these spiritual leaders who have in various degrees attained a direct vision of the spiritual problems of their age which is not given to the majority. Unlike them the average man is forced to face the spiritual problems of his time with a second-hand equipment—with the ideas and pre-conceptions that he has received from others and from his environment, and consequently his equipment is inevitably somewhat out of date owing to the time-lag in culture which is due to the slowness with which the community absorbs and appropriates new experience.

Now to-day, both as Christians and citizens, we are faced with an exceptionally difficult situation, while our outlook is limited by an historical tradition in which the original conceptions of Christian community has become weakened and obscured. We are the children of a period which marked the climax of the material prosperity and the material organization of western culture while the sense of spiritual community had reached its lowest point. The growing secularisation of culture had long since shifted the centre of men's interests from religion to practical affairs, and the traditional religious orthodoxy was felt to be no longer in harmony with modern needs.

On the other hand, the new movements and ideals which the nineteenth century had attempted to set in its place—liberalism, idealism and even positivism—had failed to satisfy men's minds, and the century had closed in doubt and disillusionment. In so far as men still believed in a spiritual community, it was not that of the historic Church but that of a universal ideal, and even this idealism no longer inspired the faith and hope which had given it such power in the days of the Enlightenment and during the early nineteenth century.

And the same decline of spiritual vitality was felt in the religious world. In Catholic Europe it was the age of *laicism* and the triumph of political anti-clericalism, while in the Protestant world the absence of persecution and the freedom and economic prosperity of the Free Churches were accompanied by a lowering of spiritual standards and a loss of spiritual vitality which narrowed and impoverished the religious tradition of Anglo-Saxon Protestantism. The uncompromising spirituality that had characterized the religious leaders of the past (whether Puritans, Quakers, or Wesleyans), had become transformed into a bourgeois cult which had come to terms with the world and was the ally and guarantee of wealth and respectability.

The result was that the whole conception of a Christian community had become faded and remote to the early twentieth century. The great words and images of the Christian past were still familiar to men's ears, but they had lost their vital significance, they had become pious phrases or antiquated metaphors. The very familiarity of the English-speaking peoples with the language of the Bible had made the average man insensitive to the profundity of its spiritual meaning. There was a gap between the universality of the ancient Christian community and the narrowness of the modern sect that is typified by the contrast between the little Bethels of the nineteenth century England and the terrible place of Jacob's vision from which they took their name.

Under these circumstances it is surely not surprising that the trend towards community in the modern world has left the Christian tradition on one side and found secular or at least non-Christian forms in which to express itself. For at the same time that the Christian tradition of community was becoming increasingly isolated and segregated from modern economic and cultural life, the world was becoming obscurely conscious of the loss of community and the need for social integration.

This movement was as a rule a movement of revolt against the nineteenth century State, because the latter had become separated from the community. The State had become either an end in itself, as in three great military bureaucratic empires, Austria, Germany and

Russia, or the legal framework of individualist society as in the capitalist States of the West. But at the same time the movement was hostile or unsympathetic to the Church, because the latter also was regarded either as an end in itself, something apart from the community, or as an ally and bulwark of capitalism. Hence it found typical expression on the Continent in revolutionary socialism which was at once anti-clerical and anti-bureaucratic as well as anti-individualist and anti-capitalist.

On the other hand the trend towards community also found expression in the nationalist movements which were an assertion of cultural and racial community, against the artificial unity of military or bureaucratic imperialism. It is true that nationalism often tends to ally itself with bureaucracy, but the spiritual appeal of both these movements lies elsewhere. It is the revolutionary appeal to an ideal community based on the brotherhood of blood or the brotherhood of the workers against the external legal compulsions which determined the relations of governors and governed, or capitalists and wage earners. The modern cult of nationality had its origin not in the national States, but among peoples who experienced the sense of national community in the midst of political servitude and division, in Poland and Ireland, in the Germany of Kleist and the Italy of Mazzini.

Moreover, nationalism was in origin by no means unfriendly to Christianity. In Ireland and Poland it drew much of its strength from the religion of the people, and in the case of Poland at least it tended to adopt a specifically Christian ideology through the Messianic mysticism of Krasinski and his contemporaries who saw their oppressed and rejected nation as the redeemer of Europe. The nationalism of Kleist and Mazzini, it is true, was not so definitely Christian, but it was very far from being secular, for it was inspired by a thoroughly religious ideal of the nation as a spiritual community.

It was not thus, however, that nationalism achieved its victory. The cause of Irish and Polish nationalism was defeated, while Germany and Italy attained their unity by the *Real-Politik* of Cavour and Bismarck who identified the cause of nationality with the victory of the military and bureaucratic State.

And in the same way the national and religious idealism of the Slavophils in Russia became the servant of the police State of Alexander III and found a purely negative expression in the repressive obscurantism of Pobedonostsev.

This period of compromise, or equilibrium between the forces of nationalism and the bureaucratic traditions of the European monarchies, lasted from about 1850 until the war of 1914–18, which destroyed the three great continental empires and set loose the impulse to community which had been confined in the strait-waistcoat of bureaucracy. The leading characteristic of all the new régimes and political movements that have arisen since 1917 has been the tendency to merge the State in the community and to assert the supremacy of the common will over every legal and constitutional limitation.

This principle found its first and perhaps most complete expression in Russia, where Communist theory deliberately taught men to regard the State as an instrument of the class war and the Communist Party, or, as Lenin crudely puts it, a bludgeon with which to beat the bourgeoisie— in other words, those individuals who refuse to merge their consciousness and their interests in those of the mass community. In Italian Fascism, this tendency is somewhat less developed owing to the fact that the juridical conception of the State is too deeply rooted in the culture and traditions of the Latin world to be easily uprooted. Accordingly the emphasis

here was on the totalitarian State rather than
in the totalitarian community.

In Germany, on the other hand, the situation
was exceptionally favourable to the development of a new ideology. The collapse of the
dynasty had discredited the traditional bureaucratic forms of the State; while, on the other
hand, the sense of national humiliation and
oppression produced by the peace of Versailles
had discredited the cosmopolitan ideals of both
Liberals and Socialists and had drawn the classes
together in a common feeling of resentment.
Moreover, the idea of a Volksgemeinschaft—of
national and racial community as something
transcending the artificial juridical forms of the
State—had behind it, as in no other country,
the prestige of a great literary and philosophic
tradition. And hence it was in Germany, rather
than in Russia or Italy, that the two different
tendencies towards Community of which I
have spoken—Nationalism and Socialism—
united to produce a new creed—that of National
Socialism.

Now if my diagnosis of the situation is correct,
it is clear that the essence of the totalitarian
régime is to be found not in dictatorship but
in mass consciousness and mass organisation.
The real conflict is not that between democracy

and dictatorship, but that between individualism and " communitarianism."

We are apt to base our political reasoning on the assumption that since England is a democratic country, therefore every democracy must conform to the Anglo-Saxon pattern. Actually the English political tradition has been aristocratic rather than democratic, and our existing social system still retains the marks of its aristocratic origins even though they are decently veiled by our democratic ideology.

Our individualism, our parliamentary form of government, and our ideals of personal freedom (not to mention our class system and our economic order), are in very large measure an inheritance that our modern urban democracy has received from the aristocratic traditions of the old rural England. The popular conception of English democracy is largely based on an interpretation or falsification of history in terms of the middle-class liberal ideology of the nineteenth century. In reality England consisted of thousands of miniature monarchies—often highly autocratic ones—ruled like the medieval State by the temporal power of the squire and the spiritual authority of the parson. English public life was for the most part confined to the rulers of these little communities who formed as it were the base of a second pyramid which culminated in the great ruling families of the Whig Oligarchy. The democratic element in this society was represented, not by the towns which were dominated by small privileged corporations, but by the religious sects which constituted a number of separate worlds, each with its own ethos and social tradition, but all based to a greater or less degree on the affirmation of spiritual freedom and autonomy. It is difficult to exaggerate the importance of this sectarian religious element in the development of English society; and the transformation of English society from an agrarian aristocracy to a plutocratic democracy in the course of the nineteenth century owes far more to their influence than is usually realized. Nevertheless the change was a very gradual one, as compared with the revolutionary transformations of the continental State, and even to-day English society and English culture preserve in countless ways the imprint of the pattern of the older society.

In short, British democracy is not Democracy in the pure state; it is a remarkable hybrid which owes its distinctive character, its virtues and its faults, to aristocratic Liberalism and nonconformist Independency. Pure democracy in the historic sense owed its origin to Rousseau and first entered European history with the French Revolution. It is the creed of the Jacobins, the followers of Robespierre and St. Just, of Billaud-Varennes and Collot d'Herbois, the men who ruled France with such terrible energy and ruthless determination that the single year of their power changed the whole course of European history.

Anyone who studies the history of the First French Republic in the light of recent political developments cannot fail to be impressed by the way in which the Jacobins anticipated practically all the characteristic features of the modern totalitarian régimes: the dictatorship of a party in the name of the community, the use of propaganda and appeals to mass emotion, as well as of violence and terrorism, the conception of revolutionary justice as a social weapon, the regulation of economic life in order to realize revolutionary ideals, and above all the attempt to enforce a uniform ideology on the whole people and the proscription and persecution of every other form of political thought.

Moreover, the Jacobin democracy of 1793-4 was not only the prototype of the totalitarian State, it was also the matrix in which the main types of modern totalitarian ideology had their origin. It was the source not only of the strict republican democratic tradition which influenced in greater or less degree all the democratic movements of modern Europe, but also of the democratic Nationalism which found its first expression in the orators of the Convention and in Socialism which derives from the economic democracy of St. Just through Babeuf and Buonarotti.

From our present point of view, however, the most important thing about this prototype of all our modern revolutionary and communitarian movements is that it also marks the decisive turning point in the relations between the State and the Christian Church. Although it finally resulted in the separation of Church and State, this was the very opposite of the ideal which it consciously aimed at. Its intention was to unite rather than to separate, to destroy the traditional dualism of the two powers and the two Societies and to reabsorb the Church in the Community. Nevertheless, this community was not a secular community in the strict sense of the word. The new republic as conceived by Robespierre and St. Just and by their master Rousseau before them was a spiritual community, based on definite moral doctrines and finding direct religious expression in an official civic cult.

At first the revolution attempted to combine the new faith with the old religion by the creation of a " Constitutional Church " separated from Rome and inseparably bound up with the new state. But the victory of the Jacobins involved the abandonment of this compromise and the institution of the religion of Nature and the Supreme Being as the official faith of the republic. The feasts of the Church were abolished in favour of the new civic festivals, Sunday made way for the Décadi, and the churches were secularized or devoted to the new cult. Thus the democratic community became a counter church of which Robespierre was at once the high priest and the grand inquisitor, while Catholicism and atheism alike were ruthlessly proscribed.

This was the boldest and most logical attempt to solve the problem of the relations of Church and State, or rather the relations of religion and society, that had been made since the Reformation, and its failure largely accounts for the collapse of the democratic experiment and the coming of a military dictatorship. For the nineteenth century opened with a reaction against the whole idea of a totalitarian democracy, a reaction which showed itself, on the one hand, in the tendency of the new nationalism to ally itself with royalism and traditional Christianity, and, on the other, in the tendency of revolutionary or progressive opinion to identify itself with the doctrine of liberal individualism.

Thus the modern English way of regarding the democratic and liberal ideologies as practically identical, falsifies the whole perspective of nineteenth century history. For the founders of nineteenth century Liberalism, such as Benjamin Constant, Mme de Stael, Royer-Collard, Guizot and de Tocqueville, were so horrified by their experience of the terrible reality of mass dictatorship that they did all they could to diminish the power and prestige of the community in favour of the individual. Hence while they were hostile to the Church as an embodiment of social authority, and to the principle of a religion of the State, they were highly sympathetic to the freedom of religious opinion and to Christianity in so far as it stood for the sovereignty of the individual conscience. Thus a Liberal like Benjamin Constant valued religion for the very reason that the Jacobins had persecuted it, i.e. because it was a separatist power. As a modern writer has said, he saw it as a sanctuary to which men might retire, as a camp in which he could entrench himself against the omnipotence of the State.

This desire to protect man's spiritual life

from the intrusion of the State, coincided with
the general tendency of Liberalism to restrict
the State to its minimal function as policeman
and keeper of the peace, which also finds
expression in economic liberalism, so that, in
contrast to the democratic State, the liberal
State is not the Community but only its inglori-
ous and necessary servant.

But such a solution was only valid so long
as the private worlds of the nineteenth century
man of business and man of letters and man
of science retained their autonomy. Nor was
this segregation of human interests into watertight compartments wholly satisfactory even
while it lasted. For religion (and literature
also) paid dearly for their freedom from State
interference by their increasing isolation and
separation from social reality. Although the
State might be regarded as the servant of the
community, it was by no means the servant of
the spiritual power, as in the Middle Ages; it was
rather the servant of material interests which
developed unguided and unchecked, in an atmosphere of spiritual anarchy. And thus the economic
development which was stimulated by the liberal
régime of free trade and free competition
ultimately proved fatal to liberalism itself. As
the modern community integrated itself into

F

a vast mechanized economic unit, it became impossible to keep the economic and the political worlds apart, and the State was forced to assume responsibility for the maintenance and smooth functioning of the economic machine.

This coming together of politics and economics involved the death of the liberal State and the emergence of a new type of community which whether we call it socialist, or democratic or fascist is essentially totalitarian since the planned organization and unitary control of the economic system inevitably means the organization and control of social activities in general.

Thus the difference between the dictatorships and the democracies is not so much one between the totalitarian and the non-totalitarian as between a Community-State that has made a deliberate breach with the old liberal tradition and is aggressively conscious of its totalitarian character, and a Community-State which has evolved gradually from the Liberal State without any violent cataclysm and which disguises its totalitarian character by a liberal ideology. The Christian community is therefore faced with similar problems in all the modern States that have attained a high degree of mechanization and economic organization. But the problem is obviously much more acute in the

dictator States with their militant mass consciousness and their ideological fanaticism than
in the liberal democracies where the minorities
still possess full legal rights and where the
survival of a liberal ideology favours religious
liberty and freedom of thought.

In both cases, however, there is the same
fundamental psychological problem of how the
individual and the minority is to resist the
pressure of mass opinion and mass emotion,
and how it is possible to reconcile spiritual
freedom and personal responsibility with the
mechanized existence of a unit in the economic
machine. No doubt the rich man, the scientist
and the politician enjoy much more freedom
under a parliamentary government than under
a dictatorship, but the average man and woman,
and still more the average boy and girl, are no
more their own masters in the one than in the
other. Their minds are moulded and their
opinions are formed insensibly by the mass
suggestion and mass propaganda of the press, the
radio and the cinema. And the only difference is
that the fascist and communist States attempt
to direct this propaganda in accordance with
their respective ideologies, whereas in the
democracies it is a soulless force which is
inspired purely by the motive of profit.

It may be argued that this was always so and that the common man has always believed what he has been told to believe. But we must remember that in the past the Christian community was itself the great maker of public opinion. The place of the modern cinema and press were taken in Catholic countries by the rites and festivals of the Church, and in Protestant ones by the Bible and the preaching of the Word. Thus the Christian faith and the Christian *Weltanschauung* formed the ideological background of all culture and social life, and it was only among the more highly educated, in the humanism of the universities and schools, that there was any conscious attempt to transcend the limits of this popular religious culture.

To-day this universal religious background of popular culture has disappeared, and even among practising Christians religion no longer occupies the same psychic territory as it did in the past. Its ideological influence is weak, even where its moral influence is still active. And this provides the new socio-political ideologies both with an opportunity and a justification. For the greatest danger that threatens modern civilization is its degeneration into a hedonistic mass civilization of the cinema, the picture paper and the dance hall, where the individual, the family and the nation dissolve into a human herd without personality, or traditions or beliefs.

This is the problem which the modern social ideologies attempt to solve by drastic and radical methods. Communism, which is the earliest of them, offers the simplest and the most radical solution, but it attains this simplicity by shutting its eyes to one half—and that the most important half—of the problem. In accordance with the Calvinistic determinism of Marx's theory of increasing misery, it sees in modern mechanized civilization only the sufferings that capitalism inflicts on the people as workers and not the new luxury that it offers to them as consumers. It ignores the existence of the new bourgeoisie that has grown up between the capitalist and the manual labourer and which is the dominant social type in all the western democracies. And this one-sidedness has been accentuated by the fact that Communism found its field of action in Russia, the most backward of European countries, where the new mechanized civilization was practically non-existent, and where the vast majority of the population still lived in the pre-industrial world of peasant culture. Hence on the one hand Communism in Russia was able to idealize a material civilization that it had not yet experienced and on the other, owing to the apparently inexhaustible reserves of vitality stored up in the virgin soil of the peasant population, it could use its human resources as wastefully and unregardingly as nineteenth century America exploited the natural resources of her boundless territories.

Thus Communism hitherto has concentrated on the creation of a totalitarian economic system and has not given much attention to the sociological problem of how an already mechanized society is to be physically revitalized and morally reinvigorated. This is the problem which Fascism and especially National Socialism have expressly undertaken to solve, and their success as against liberal democracy depends far less on their foreign policy than on whether or no they are able to succeed on this sociological and psychological home front. The essential problem is how to transform the mechanized dehumanized mass population of an industrialized State into a true community with a common ethos and a common faith.

Now in the first place Fascism, like Communism though in a more deliberate way, has had resort to forcible measures of social discipline, the same method that has been used

from time immemorial to transform an unorganized mob into an army. This is the aspect
of Fascism which is most distasteful to the
English for whom the army in a sense stands
outside the State: but obviously the case
is entirely different on the Continent, and
especially in Prussia, where the army formed
the core of the political organism from the
beginning.

Accordingly in Germany this aspect of Fascism
may be taken for granted and the essential
characteristic of National Socialism is to be
found rather in its attempt to create an ideology
which will be the soul of the new State and
which will co-ordinate the new resources of
propaganda and mass suggestion in the interests
of the national community. This is the most
deliberate attempt that has been made since
the French Revolution to fill the vacuum which
has been created by the disappearance of the
religious background of European culture and
the secularization of social life by nineteenth
century liberalism. It is a new form of natural
religion, not the rationalized natural religion of
the eighteenth century, but a mystical neo-
paganism which worships the forces of nature
and life and the spirit of the race as already
manifested in the heroic dead and the living

nation, and as about to be perfected in the ideal racial community of the future. Thus the Nazi revolution is conceived as a kind of popular Nordic Renaissance; a reassertion of the native traditions and instincts of the race against the successive importations of alien culture from the Mediterranean south and the Semitic and Slavonic east.

And so the anti-Semitic policy of National Socialism is to be explained as a deliberate attempt to focus this sentiment of reaction on a definite social figure: to make the Jew the representative and the scapegoat of the mechanical, cosmopolitan, urban mass civilization which is the antithesis of an organic national culture.

Thus in its ideological content National Socialism does not differ very widely from the nationalist movements of the past. Where it differs from them is that what was formerly the romantic dream of poets and idealists—like Kleist and Arndt and Adam Müller, or the Slavophils in Russia, or Sinn Fein in Ireland—has become a psychological instrument of the totalitarian State for the control and unification of mass opinion.

But there remains an internal contradiction between the idea of the nation as a spiritual

community and that of a totalitarian dictatorship—between the Church State and the police
State—which vitiates the religious idealism of
the Nazi cult. It is impossible to revive the old
northern ethics of heroism and honour by the
secret police and the official press. The heroic
idealism of Hölderlin and Beethoven, of Wagner
and Nietzsche, withers in an atmosphere of
propaganda and repression as the humanitarian
idealism of Rousseau perished in the bloody
shambles of the Terror.

In short the chief evils of the totalitarian
State are due not to its ideals, but to the methods
that are used to enforce them, and these
methods, which were in fact first applied in
Russia, can be used to enforce any ideals,
even democratic ones.

The democrat is faced by the same essential
problem as the Communist and the Fascist:
viz. the creation of a living community out
of the confusion of material interests and selfish
particularisms that have grown up with modern
civilization; and if he has so far escaped
the sacrifice of freedom which the other systems
involve, it may be due less to the superiority
of his ideals than to the fact that the western
democracies have been sheltered from the full
impact of the new forces by the wealth and

power that they had acquired in the previous age.

Nevertheless we must remember that it was actually under democratic auspices that the totalitarian State made its first appearance nearly 150 years ago in France, and as that farseeing Liberal, de Tocqueville, pointed out more than a century ago in his study of democracy in America, the power of mass opinion exercises a more universal and irresistible tyranny over the individual mind in a democratic society than the most authoritarian of dictatorships. Hitherto the chief safeguard of personal liberty in democratic society has been the anarchy and disorder of capitalist individualism, but if that anarchy is to be replaced by a collective order, the resultant democratic State may be no less totalitarian in character than Italian Fascism or German National Socialism.

Thus the problem that we have to face in Great Britain to-day is how to transform our disordered society into a living community without sacrificing the old liberal-democratic ideals of freedom and humanity. We have already gone further in this direction than either France or the United States by the organization of the social services and the

public control of economic life. We have
already discarded economic liberalism in favour
of a sort of national socialism, which is
however of an entirely different type from
that of the totalitarian States of the Continent. Our nationalism, though it is far
stronger than we realize, is more traditional
than that of Germany, less bound up with
racial dogmas and more tolerant of the rights
of others. And in the same way our socialism
is also less revolutionary and more adaptable
than the socialism of continental Europe. It
has a strong element of religious idealism which
it inherits from the Christian Socialism and
Christian liberalism of nineteenth century
England.

On the other hand, we must admit that the
spirit of our society still remains predominantly
capitalistic. If we have less autocracy than
the continental countries, we have more pluto-
cracy, and the plutocratic tradition with its
competitiveness, its snobbery and its social
exclusivism is more opposed to the spirit of
community than dictatorship itself. But we
cannot transform a plutocratic imperialism
into a democratic community merely by an
extension of government control and a more
intensive system of bureaucratic organisation,

for this only increases that pressure of social mechanism on human life and spiritual freedom which is the greatest evil of modern civilization. The totalitarian States recognize this in so much as they emphasize the importance of a new ideology, which shall serve as the spiritual foundation of their reconstruction of society. But if this ideology is itself an artificial system imposed by force and propaganda on the popular mind it only involves further inroads on spiritual freedom and an increasing mechanization of life.

No doubt it is easier to collectivize society if it is possible to eliminate everything that does not conform to the simple creed of a party, but the spiritual life of a democratic community ought to be richer and not poorer than that of an individualist State, otherwise collectivization means the spiritual impoverishment of society and the loss of the higher cultural values. The possibility of realizing the ideal of a free community depends in the long run on whether it is possible for it to offer men a richer and deeper spiritual life than that of the individualistic culture of the past. Apart from this, the totalitarian State will be a servile and mechanical mass organization, whether it claims to serve the interests of the proletariat, the nation or the race. In other words the transformation of the economic and political machine into the organ of a free and living community can only come from within by a change of spirit.

Now it is impossible to consider this problem of the spiritual re-ordering of life apart from religion, for it is the very task with which religion has always been concerned; and if in the immediate past religion has confined itself to the life of the individual, this is not because the spiritual life of society was a matter of indifference to the Church but because the organization of social life proceeded from below and took no account of spiritual problems and needs.

But this state of affairs was a highly exceptional one and cannot be regarded as typical either from an historical or a theological point of view. As I said at the beginning, we cannot derive much help from the conditions of yesterday, when the influence of religion on society was reduced to a minimum by the spiritual division and intellectual anarchy of individualistic culture. It is more instructive to turn back to Christian origins, for there in the age of the Roman Empire, in spite of the vast differences of culture and external conditions, we find a remarkable parallel to the situation of the modern world.

The Roman Empire was faced by the same vital problem as Europe to-day. Its relatively high standard of material civilization had become a source of vital degeneration rather than of social progress. The life was passing out of the old City-State and its institutions, and in its place there had arisen a standardized cosmopolitan civilization inspired by no higher motive than mass hedonism. The State-provided pleasures of the baths, the circus and the amphitheatre gave the majority the luxuries that had formerly been the privilege of the few, and compensated them for the loss of civic freedom and honour. The citizen need no longer be a soldier, for he could pay the peasant and the barbarian to serve as mercenaries and he need no longer work, for that was the business of the slaves. And so the land decayed and the cities multiplied, producing everywhere from the Atlantic to the Euphrates the same pattern of social life—a leisure State in which the Mediterranean peoples gradually lost their vital energy and became sterile and senile.

To this world Christianity came not as an ideology which should provide a basis for social reconstruction and reform, but as a new light appearing suddenly in a dark place. The appeal of Christianity lay in its absolute

otherness and its complete forgiveness. It was
something that the civilized world of Greece
and Rome could not produce from itself or
by its own power, it was deliverance from the
world by a power coming from without: "the
Dayspring from on high that has visited us,
to give light to them that sit in darkness and
in the shadow of death: to guide our feet into the
way of peace."

And so while the legions marched down the
straight road, and the city populace thronged
the theatres of Gadara, the unknown Son of
Man sat apart on a mountain and spoke words
of new life to the elect gathered at random
from the fishermen of the lake and the peasants
and craftsmen of the villages. This new word
was of a different order to the philosophies and
ideologies of men. It recreated the world from
within, silently and irresistibly filling the waste
places of the human soul which had been left derelict in the external advance of material civilization. And in the same way the new community,
which was the organ and vehicle of this living
word, was a community of a different order
from the kingdoms and societies of men. It
did not meet Caesar on his own ground or
give a direct answer to the national demands
of the Jewish people. It was the divine seed

of a new world miraculously springing up in a world that seemed worn out and under sentence of death.

Can this miracle be repeated in a world that has for the second time grown old? Can the Word of Life once more enlighten the darkness of a civilization that is infinitely richer and more powerful than that of pagan Rome but which seems equally to have lost its sense of direction and to be threatened with social degeneration and spiritual disintegration?

It is obvious that the Christian must answer in the affirmative. Yet on the other hand he must not look for a quick and easy solution to a problem on which the whole future of humanity depends. At the present time when every political party, even the Communist International, is attempting to enlist the forces of organized Christianity in a Common Front against its political opponents, there is a great danger that Christians should take the line of least resistance and acquiesce in some facile synthesis of their religion with the dominant ideology. But it is no less dangerous for Christians to go to the other extreme, to preach a kind of Christian totalitarianism which would make Christianity a rival to modern social ideologies on their own ground. I do not reject the possibility of a Christian State even in the sense of a Christian totalitarian State, though that seems hardly conceivable at the present day. What is inherently impossible is any identification or fusion of the Church with the political community, for each possesses its own formal principle without which it would no longer be itself. The State, whether national, socialist or democratic, exists for the people, and by the people, but the Church exists for the Divine Word and Spirit of which it is the organ.

Modern society is obscurely conscious of its need for recreation and rebirth and is groping in a blind and instinctive way after life and light. Yet it has not sufficient time to look far or dig deep. It is forced to lay hold of whatever materials lie ready to hand in order to construct some hastily improvised system to meet the need of the moment. And since the power which guides this work of reconstruction—the political party—is itself the creator of social circumstance, the process of unifying the divided aims and consciousness of the community must inevitably be destructive and incomplete.

The Church, on the other hand, is not concerned with finding immediate solutions for pressing social problems. The time factor indeed is almost irrelevant, for it is the society of the

G

world to come. It is not, like the State, a social engineer, but the guardian of the waters of life, and its essential task is to keep the sources pure and inviolate. Thus, though the totalitarian State may absorb or eliminate all the secondary activities of the Church, it can never compete with it on its own ground which lies at a deeper level of man's being. No doubt the politician tends to undervalue or to ignore the importance of religion and the reality of the religious values. Nevertheless the more of a statesman he is, the more will he recognise the limitations of political action, and will realize that even the State itself gains more than it loses by the existence of an autonomous society which serves the deepest needs of humanity, and which forms the channel by which supernatural life flows into humanity, transforming and renewing it from within as the divine seed of a new spiritual creation.

IV

CONSIDERATIONS ON THE CORONATION OF AN ENGLISH KING

IV

CONSIDERATIONS ON THE CORONATION OF AN ENGLISH KING

I

THE Coronation represents the most solemn and definite consecration of the State to Religion that we can conceive. Does it mean what it says or is it a gigantic piece of bluff—the consecration of a power that no longer exists, to a faith in which we no longer believe?

I am afraid this is a question that the English mind is unwilling to face. We react instinctively and emotionally to the great pageant that flatters our national pride and yet at the same time appeals to something deeper or higher, some vague numinous conception of the State as a holy community and of political power as a sacred God-given office which transcends the limit of utilitarian and nationally selfish ends, and binds man by a golden chain to the order of heaven. But we shirk the effort of analysing and criticizing these emotional reactions in the light of reason. Better, no doubt, that we should do so than that we should sacrifice wisdom to logic and reduce the rich confusion of our intuitive perception to a shallow and impoverished rationalism; but better still to face reality and to recognize the full implications of our social attitude, even though it involves the uncovering of hidden conflicts of will and confusions of thought.

The trouble is that it is impossible either to take the Coronation at its face value or to dismiss it as mere organized hypocrisy. We cannot hide from ourselves that the whole situation of Western culture has completely changed since the Coronation rite was produced as a natural and organic expression of the European ideal of a Christian State. Culture has been secularized, society has been secularized, and if the State in England has not been secularized it is an anomalous and exceptional phenomenon, which foreigners may be excused for regarding as an archaic survival.

When this rite was created, an atheist was an almost fabulous monster who would have been hunted down like a wild beast—even a couple of centuries ago the atheist lived a furtive, underground existence like a criminal. To-day, on the other hand, he has obtained full rights of citizenship in the Western world. A man can

be an atheist in the full sense of the word and
yet be a full partner in the State and the
common life of society. He can feel that it is
his society and *his* State just as much as they
are the Christian's; indeed even more so,
for the Christian must necessarily feel himself a
bit out of touch with the modern world, as being
bound by laws and beliefs which the majority
of his fellows do not share, while the atheist
can be a hundred per cent modern man without
having to make any reserves or withdrawals,
except on these rare occasions like the Coronation, when the old Christian order suddenly
puts its head above the surface of life and
claims a share of men's attention for a passing
moment. And when I say an atheist of course
I do not mean a man who has speculative doubts
in the existence of God, but a man who bases
his whole life and thought on the absence
of God and the godlessness of the universe,
as the Christian and the Moslem do upon His
presence and His divine Providence.

That is one side of things. But on the other
hand we have to take account of the persistence
in the world to-day of a Christian tradition,
vague and diffused no doubt, but nevertheless
living and real. It is not merely that people
continue to write letters to *The Times* expressing

surprise and indignation that a Christian country or a Christian civilization should tolerate this, that or the other. It is far more that those who realize most clearly that our civilization is not Christian or who are not even professed Christians themselves, should still feel a sense of loss and discomfort as though there was something missing, something disordered in this state of society, even though they do not feel it in their private lives.

This state of things is characteristic of the whole of European society, in spite of the different attitudes taken up by the various States. At one end of the scale stands England, still representing the traditional form of a Christian monarchy, possessing a State Church which almost alone in Europe still preserves the tithes and endowments and the privileged position of the medieval territorial Church. At the other is Russia which alone in Europe has officially recognized godlessness and has reorganized its cultural and intellectual life on atheistic principles. Between these two extremes we have every type of religio-political order, from the monarchies which approximate more or less to the English type, through the States which give juridical recognition to religion by the system of concordats, down to the laicized

States which treat religion as purely a matter of individual opinion and severely restrict its corporate manifestations.

Nevertheless, under all these diverse conditions, there lies the same fundamental situation of a secularized culture which still retains manifold traces of its Christian past, and which fails to satisfy the needs of the human conscience. For England is certainly not so Christian as its official formularies assume it to be, while even Russia is probably far less materialistic than Communist theory demands. We are not, so far as I know, undergoing a great religious revival, nor is there one in prospect, but religion has come to have much greater significance in the eyes of politicians and publicists than it had thirty years ago.

We have ceased to believe that religion and politics can be kept in watertight compartments; if they are to be entirely separated, it can only be by a surgical operation, as in Spain in 1936, by fire and sword, and if one of the two dies under the operation it is as likely to be the State as the Church. The theory of totalitarian revolution, which was so strong in Spain, demands the destruction not so much of capitalism but of the State itself, and the Church is attacked not because it is the ally of capitalism, but because it is the visible embodiment of Authority. Bakunin's Statutes of the International Alliance of Socialist Democracy (which is to the Anarchist what the Communist Manifesto is to Communism) demands "the destruction of every State and every Church together with all their various institutions, their religious, political, judicial and financial regulations, the police system, all university regulations, all social and economic regulations whatsoever, so that the millions of poor human beings who are now being cheated and gagged, tormented and exploited, delivered from the cruellest of official directors and officious clergy, from all collective and individual tyranny, would for once be able to breathe freely."

This is one solution of the spiritual conflict of the modern world—"destroy the great guilty city and give us peace"—but there is the other solution—that which is suggested in the Coronation rite—the consecration of the city of Man as the temporal representative and organ of the City of God. This solution may seem far removed from the realities of the modern world, but unless the modern world can reorientate itself in that direction there is no half-way house which is safe against the passionate

conviction of the revolutionary idealist, who
has a negative sense of absolute values, and
sees through the hollowness and shams of
secular civilization.

The nineteenth century did possess such a
half-way house in the form of Liberalism. It
started off by being badly frightened by the
menace of revolution, for it took Europe a very
long time to recover from the shock it had
received in the days of the Jacobin Reign of
Terror. On the other hand the attempt of the
romantics to restore the religious conception of
the State and to return to medieval social ideals,
shocked the rationalism of the intelligentsia and
the common sense of the middle classes, who
were dazzled by the brilliant material promise
of free trade and free competition. So the age
found the solution for its social and intellectual
problems in the Liberal compromise: individual
freedom in politics, in economics and in religion
—freedom of opinion and freedom of trade—
faith in progress and moral idealism without
metaphysical certainty or Christian dogma.

There is no need to go into the causes of
the failure of this compromise. I believe myself,
as I have argued in *Progress and Religion*
and elsewhere, that it was essentially a tran-
sitional phenomenon—a kind of twilight state

between the old Christian world and the new secular civilization. But even if we believe, as Croce does, that Liberalism possesses its own autonomous principle of life and can afford to stand on its own merits, we must still admit that it is a much more fragile and artificial construction than the nineteenth-century Liberals themselves believed it to be.

They thought that the Liberal régime was the natural state of mankind: you had only to diffuse enough useful knowledge and remove the barriers of ignorance and privilege for man to be a good Liberal. It was unthinkable that he would go back from Parliamentary institutions to monarchy, from Free Trade to Protection, from free competition to State-regulated industry, from free thought to State religion and the proscription of unorthodox opinion.

But they were wrong: all these things have happened and are happening, and even in the countries where there is as yet no dictatorship, Liberalism is a dying power. What the non-dictatorial States stand for to-day is not Liberalism but Democracy, a very different thing, as the old Liberals themselves recognized and as their last representative, Croce still points out to-day. Liberalism stands for the rights of the individual and the freedom of private opinion and private interests, while Democracy stands for the rights of the majority and the sovereignty of public opinion and the common interest. Democracy has quite abandoned the unfriendly and suspicious attitude to the State that was characteristic of Liberalism. It no longer attempts to confine its activities to the external relations of life—the preservation of peace and order—and to guard jealously against State intervention in social and economic life. It still rejects the paternalism of the old authoritarian Christian State, but it is quite ready to treat the State as a sort of universal aunt and to welcome its intrusion into the most intimate relations of life. But there remains one side of life to which the democratic State has not yet gained access. For Democracy agrees with Liberalism in its opposition to any State intervention or interference in religion, except in a purely negative way. Religion is still treated as a purely private thing—a matter of personal opinion which is left to the individual conscience.

Actually, however, there is far less justification for this attitude than there was in the age of Liberalism. For the Liberal the spiritual centre of gravity was in the individual, and the

realm of private opinion and private interests
was the ideal world. Hence, when the Liberal
spoke of religion as a purely private matter it
was in compliment rather than in derogation.
To separate the Church from the State—to
keep religion out of politics, was to elevate it
to the higher sphere of spiritual values. But
to-day in the democratic world, these values
have been reversed. The individual life has
lost its spiritual primacy, and it is social life
which now has the higher prestige, so that to
treat religion as a purely individual and personal
matter is to deprive it of actuality and to
degrade it to a lower level of value and potency.
To keep religion out of public life is to shut it
up in a stuffy Victorian back drawing-room
with the aspidistras and the antimacassars,
when the streets are full of life and youth.
And the result is that the religion of the Church
becomes increasingly alienated from real life,
while democratic society creates a new religion
of the street and the forum to take its place.

II

The most important examples of this new
type of religion or pseudo-religion which appeals
directly to the social conscience and finds

its expression in the field of politics and economics, are Socialism and Nationalism. These new creeds arose in the Liberal age—in the spiritual void that Liberalism had created by its secularization of social life, and they grew until they have not only destroyed Liberalism but have come to threaten Democracy itself, in so far as Democracy is to be identified with Parliamentarism and representative institutions, i.e. the elements that are common to Democracy and Liberalism.

Now from many points of view these new public religions are opposed to Christian traditions and morals and beliefs. At the worst they are anti-Christian and godless; at the best they assert the primacy of the temporal and set the interests of class or race or State above the needs of the human soul. They are secular religions—religions of this world. Nevertheless, they have many of the characteristics of a genuine religion. Indeed in one important respect they are more religious than the religion of the average modern Christian. They refuse to divide life. They demand that the whole of life shall be devoted and dedicated to that social end which they regard as supremely valuable. And consequently the Christian is handicapped in his resistance to their claim, because he cannot help feeling that they are, in however mistaken a way, aiming at the subordination of material things and selfish interests to a higher end—in other words they are in a fashion asserting the need for the reconsecration of social life.

This tendency works in two ways. In the first place it makes for the extension of the State—the unification of life by the State so that no room is left for the autonomous activity of the Church, and every side of human life is absorbed and incorporated into one totalitarian society. But on the other hand this tendency is hostile to the State itself regarded in the traditional way as a limited juridical society. For the State now becomes absorbed and transformed into a new kind of social organism which, in some respects, resembles a Church rather than a State, since it is based on a common faith and derives its power from organized emotion rather than from legal sovereignty.

This absorption or elimination of the State is most clearly recognized by the Communists, who have made it a dogma of their creed, but it is implicit in all the democratic or post-democratic creeds, which exalt the State only in so far as it is the organ of the racial and national community to which their devotion is really directed. For Democracy means not merely the emancipation of individuals or classes, it means the conscious self-realization of society itself. In the past, the life of the community was a reservoir of unconscious forces from which the juridical order of the State drew its power and energy. Each class was a little closed world that followed its traditional pattern of life, while the statesmen and diplomats conducted the elaborate rationalized game of politics on the social surface. To-day, however, the barriers of these separate worlds have been broken down, and the forces that lay beneath the surface of the social consciousness have acquired control. They have destroyed the prestige of the old Liberal humanist culture which was essentially an aristocratic tradition, and are creating a new civilization governed by mass emotion and inspired by mass idealism.

Thus the great religious problem of the present age is not the problem of the relation of Church and State in the traditional sense of two parallel and complementary societies which respectively order and guide the temporal and spiritual life of the community so that the latter only attains social consciousness through and in

H

them. It is the problem of how religion is to survive in a single Community which is neither Church nor State, which recognizes no formal limits, no barriers of class privilege or individual rights, but which covers the whole of life and claims to be the source and end of every human activity.

There are two obvious solutions. One is that religion should treat this universal community as something external and alien, as the Christian Church treated the pagan world, and as the Orthodox Church to-day treats the Communist State in Russia. But such a solution is only possible in so far as the new community falls short of its purpose in creating a unitary mass civilization.

Under modern conditions the existence of a hostile minority organization, even of a purely spiritual kind, becomes impossible as soon as the community has achieved conscious direction of the total activities of its members. For modern education and propaganda give the community such control over the thought and emotion of the individual, that religious emotion and belief no longer have free play. The inner world of spiritual experience has been opened up by the child psychologist and the school-master and has become public property, so that the child can literally no longer call its soul its own.

There remains the other solution—that religion shall itself permeate social life and become the ruling spirit of the new mass civilization and the totalitarian community. This was the ideal of medieval Christendom, when the Catholic Church was the universal community and the State was nothing but its temporal organ and instrument. But between medieval Christendom and modern Europe there lie four centuries of religious disunion, during which religion became a principle of division and strife instead of the cornerstone of social unity. Hence the secularization of public life of which I have already spoken and the relegation of religion to the private world of the individual conscience. And consequently the new religions which are unifying the world to-day have arisen independently, if not in hostility, to the Christian tradition. Instead of uniting men as Christianity did, by that which is highest—by faith in Christ and the fellowship of the Holy Spirit—they have appealed to the lowest common factors— to class interest, or the physical unity of blood and race, so that they cast out the devils of selfishness and avarice only to enthrone the prince of this world and the powers of darkness.

Nevertheless, as I said at the beginning, the secularization of European civilization is still incomplete. There is an inherited tradition of Christian thought and morals which has become weakened and dissipated, but which is still far from negligible. The average Socialist is not necessarily a materialist in the style of Marx, nor the average Nazi a neo-pagan of the school of Ludendorff. They are still open to Christian influences on one side of their mentality and consequently there is room for an inter-mediate solution which would still leave a place for religion and the Church in the life of the community. This solution may be called the solution of the Concordat, if we use the word not merely in the strict juridical sense in which it is used by the canonists, but so as to cover also any working system of limited co-operation between the Church and the secular community. In theory, of course, the Concordat is a treaty between two sovereign independent powers defining their mutual relations and rights; in practice to-day, even in its full juridical form, it implies little more than a recognition on the part of the State that the Church is fulfilling a legitimate social function within

certain definite limits, and a willingness on the
part of the Church to co-operate with the State
in its educational and social activities.

Of course the form of relation differs widely
according to the nature of the political régime
and the religious organization. In the case of
the established churches—Anglican, Lutheran
or Orthodox—the concordatory relation is based
on a kind of legal fiction which ignores the
secularization of modern society, and continues
to apply the traditional formulas of the Christian
past in a social order which has long ceased to
be bound by Christian principles and beliefs.
In the case of the Free Churches, on the other
hand, the juridical relation to the State is
reduced to a minimum and the Church is conceived as a voluntary association which co-exists
with other similar associations within a common
society, and co-operates with these other
associations in the service of the community.
Finally we have the Catholic Church, which in
some societies approximates to the position of
an established Church, and in others to that of a
Free Church, but which in either case attempts,
whenever it is possible, to define its relation
to the State in the strict juridical form of an
explicit Concordat.

This is admittedly an imperfect solution, but

it is the only one that is appropriate to the imperfect state of our secularized civilization, and consequently it is better than a perfect solution which has no relation to the realities of the modern world. The religious idealist sees in a Concordat a bargain between a corrupt church and a tyrannical government in which the interests of both religion and freedom are sacrificed to worldly interests. He dreads above all to see the Church enlisted on the side of law and order as a kind of auxiliary police force. But this danger was really far greater under the old régime of State establishments, when the Gallican Church was the servant of the monarchy and the Anglican Church the ally of the squirearchy, than it is to-day; and it was by the Concordat or the concordatory system that the Church was liberated from this confusion of temporal and spiritual relations. The principle of the Concordat goes back behind Napoleon and behind Constantine to the New Testament, where an intense conviction of the opposition between the Christian Church and the pagan world in no way militates against the acceptance of the State (even of the Roman Empire under Nero) as a God-given order to which the Christian owes not only external submission but active loyalty. The Church's real enemy is not the

State but the World; that is to say secular
civilization considered as a closed order which
shuts out God from human life and deifies its
own power and wealth.

At the present day this spirit of the World is
stronger than ever. It is becoming fully self-
conscious and threatens to absorb the State
and to constitute itself as the universal order
of human life—a Church-State which would
be the Kingdom of Antichrist. And hence the
Christian Church to-day is the ally of the
State in a new sense, because it is only so long
as the State continues to exist as something
separate from the community—an organization
with definite functions and limited responsi-
bilities—that the Church itself can maintain
its right to exist. The elimination of the State
involves the elimination of the Church and its
absorption into the totalitarian community.
This is what has happened in the U.S.S.R.
where the State is regarded as the transitory
instrument by which the Communist super-
State eliminates all separate social forms and
interests, and it is tending to be the case in
Germany where the attempt to reach a Concordat with the Church has broken down owing
to the all-embracing claims of the racial community which includes and transcends the

State. Only in Italy do we find a totalitarian system which accepts the idea of the State in its classical legal form, and there consequently it is also possible to retain the concordatory relation with the Church in a strict juridical form.

But it is important to remember that the acceptance of a Concordat with the State ought not to involve the withdrawal of the Church from social life or the adoption of a passive quietist type of Christianity. It is no longer possible for religion to confine itself to the inner world of the individual conscience and private religious experience, any more than it is possible for the State to confine itself to its functions as the guardian of public order.

As the modern State has become democratic, so modern Christianity must become communal and break down the old barriers that separated religion from life. Of course there is the danger that as religion penetrates social life, it will itself become not merely socialized but secularized. The Church's task is not to become a competitor with the State in its social action but to find new social means of expression for its spiritual action. The Church remains what she has always been, the organ of the Divine Word and the channel of Divine Grace. It is her mission to transform the world by bringing every side of human existence and every human activity into contact with the sources of supernatural life. Even the modern State, that new Leviathan, that "King over all the children of pride," is not irrelevant to the work of grace nor impenetrable to its influence. If it does not destroy itself, it must be transformed and reconsecrated, as the power of the barbarian warrior became transfigured into the sacred office of a Christian King.

V

CHRISTIANITY AND POLITICS

V

CHRISTIANITY AND POLITICS

NOTHING could be more discouraging to the man or woman who believes in the need for applying Christian principles to social and political life than the present state of the world and the present political outlook.

We see everywhere the threat of war and the race for rearmament.

We see the collapse of the humanitarian ideals of the League of Nations, collective security, the reign of law and the outlawry of war, in which so many Christians (chiefly, it is true, Protestants but also many Catholics) have put their trust during the last twenty years. We see war in China, war in Spain, the danger of war in Central Europe and the threat of civil strife in France.

We see everywhere the appeal to naked force against individual and group rights : Communist ideals realizing themselves in mass execution and the ruthless suppression of minorities; the ruthless suppression of minority opinion in Central Europe ; the persecution of the Jews ;

while those who disapprove of all this give either open or veiled approval to religious persecution in Spain.

Finally the Catholic social experiment of a Christian corporate State in Austria has been blotted out and the Catholics have accepted their defeat, while the victory of the Catholic cause in Spain has been accomplished by a resort to the same use of force which has led to the suppression of Catholic Action elsewhere.

All this is a terrible blow both to the idealists who believed in the triumph of peace and justice by the good will of the peoples, and also to the rationalists who thought that the world had outgrown war and national rivalry and that the time had come for a planned scientific social order, which would be democratic and international and humanitarian.

But ought it to be a blow to Christians, too? Have we any reason to believe that a Christian social order could be immediately realized here and now? Have we any reason to suppose that the right side necessarily wins? Or if we believe that it must win eventually, must it win this time, in this particular age and these particular circumstances? And finally, have we any right to suppose that history will proceed according to plan, that it will realize the hopes and ideals of men? In other words, is history a reasonable process or is it essentially incalculable and irrational?

Now it seems to me that the Christian is bound to believe that there is a spiritual purpose in history—that it is subject to the designs of Providence and that somehow or other God's will is done. But that is a very different thing from saying that history is rational in the ordinary sense of the word. There are, as it were, two levels of rationality, and history belongs to neither of them. There is the sphere of completely rationalized human action—the kind of rationality that we get in a balance sheet or in the plans and specifications of an architect or an engineer. And there is the higher sphere of rationality to which the human mind attains, but which is not created by it— the high realities of philosophy and abstract truth.

But between these two realms there is a great intermediate region in which we live, the middle earth of life and history; and that world is submitted to forces which are both higher and lower than reason. There are forces of nature in the strict sense and there are higher forces of spiritual good and evil which we cannot measure. Human life is essentially a warfare

against unknown powers—not merely against
flesh and blood, which are themselves irrational
enough, but against principalities and powers,
against "the Cosmocrats of the Dark Aeon,"
to use St. Paul's strange and disturbing
expression; powers which are more than rational
and which make use of lower things, things
below reason, in order to conquer and rule
the world of man.

Of course if we were pure spirits, the whole
process of history and human life might be
intelligible and spiritually transparent. We
should be like a man in calm weather on a clear
tropical lagoon who can look down and see the
lower forms of life in their infinite variety and
the powers of evil like the sharks that move
silently and powerfully through the clear water,
and who can also look up and see the ordered
march of the stars.

But this is not given to man. The actor in
history is like the captain who sees nothing but
clouds above and waves below, who is driven
by the wind and the current. He must trust
in his chart and his compass, and even these
cannot deliver him from the blind violence of
the elements. If he makes a mistake, or if
the chart fails him, he dies in a blind flurry
of dark water and with him the crew who have

no responsibility except to obey orders and to trust their officers.

It is true that the theologian and the philosopher aspire to the spiritual state but they only attain to it partially and momentarily; for the rest of their lives, outside their science, they belong to the world of other men. But the politician and the man of action are like the sailor, and the State is like the ship which may be wrecked by an error of a single man; and it makes no difference if it is a democracy or a dictatorship, just as it makes no difference whether the ship is sailed by the owner or whether the captain is chosen by the officers and the officers by the crew.

It seems the very nature of history that individuals and apparently fortuitous events have an incalculable effect upon the fortunes of the whole society. As Burke wrote: "It is often impossible to find any proportion between the apparent force of any moral cause or any assigned, and their known operation. We are therefore obliged to deliver up their operation to mere chance, or more piously (perhaps more rationally) to the occasional interposition and the irresistible hand of the Great Disposer. The death of a man at a critical juncture, his disgust, his retreat, his disgrace, have brought

ɪ

innumerable calamities on a whole nation. A common soldier, a child, a girl at the door of an inn have changed the face of the future and almost of Nature."[1]

This has always been so, but it is seen in the most striking way when it comes to a question of moralizing politics or realizing social ideals in practice. It is here that we see most clearly and tragically the contradiction between human aims and historical results and the way in which fate seems to bring so much that is best in social endeavour to sterility or to disaster. Take two examples from the period of modern history which I happen to have been studying of late. First frustration of social idealism. The great Revolution a hundred and fifty years ago was a deliberate attempt to moralize political relations and to create a new order based on moral principles which would vindicate the human rights of every individual whatever his economic or social position. Under the guidance of men who believed most wholeheartedly in these ideals, it led nevertheless to as complete a subversion and denial of those rights as it is possible to conceive. It led to the denial of freedom of conscience and freedom of opinion; it led to terrorism and wholesale judicial murder,

[1] Letters on the Regicide Peace., ed.: E. J. Payne, p. 6.

until every man of principles, whatever his principles were, had been exterminated or outlawed, and society returned with gratitude and relief to the absolute dictatorship of an unscrupulous military despot. For Bonaparte appeared to his contemporaries as an angel of light in comparison with the idealists and social reformers who, instead of creating a Utopia, had made a hell on earth.

In the second place, to take an example from the opposite side, there is the case of the war in La Vendée which brings up both the question of the just war and that of the conscientious objector. The men of La Vendée had every justification for their resistance to the revolutionary government, since it had clearly violated the rights of freedom of opinion and religious liberty that were laid down in the constitution, and since the latter expressly admitted the right of the citizen to resist the government in such cases. The actual occasion of the rising was moreover the question of military service in defence of the revolution against which the men of La Vendée had a direct and simple conscientious objection. Hence the war in La Vendée which was at once a just war if ever there was one and a case of spontaneous popular resistance to compulsory service in what they considered an unjust war.

Yet what was the result? Instead of sending 12,000 conscripts to the army, of whom a small proportion would have been killed or wounded, the whole population was involved in the most desperate struggle that any people ever experienced: a struggle which is said to have cost nearly a quarter of a million lives, which caused practically every town and village and farm to be destroyed, and which contributed largely, if indirectly, to the horrors of the Reign of Terror in the rest of France. And so their desire to keep out of a war they did not approve of caused another war of a far more atrocious kind, and their determination to vindicate their just rights led to every kind of injustice and cruelty.

These are extreme instances, but all through history we find plentiful evidence of the same non-moral and irrational tendency which causes idealists and humanitarians to despair. And at the present day humanitarianism and moral idealism have become so much a part of our tradition that Christians often unconsciously or even consciously accept the same point of view and are tempted to despair by the failure of Christian ideals to work out in practice.

Actually, however, Christianity has never accepted these postulates, and the Christian ought to be the last person in the world to lose hope in the presence of the failure of the right and the apparent triumph of evil. For all this forms part of the Christian view of life, and the Christian discipline is expressly designed to prepare us to face such a situation.

Christianity, to a far greater degree than any other religion, is a historical religion and it is knit up inseparably with the living process of history. Christianity teaches the existence of a divine progress in history which will be realized through the Church in the Kingdom of God. But at the same time it recognizes the essential duality of the historical process—the co-existence of two opposing principles, each of which works and finds concrete social expression in history. Thus we have no right to expect that Christian principles will work in practice in the simple way that a political system may work. The Christian order is a supernatural order. It has its own principles and its own laws which are not those of the visible world and which may often seem to contradict them. Its victories may be found in apparent defeat and its defeats in material success.

We see the whole thing manifested clearly

and perfectly once and once only, i.e. in the life of Jesus, which is the pattern of the Christian life and the model of Christian action. The life of Jesus is profoundly historical; it is the culminating point of thousands of years of living historical tradition. It is the fulfilment of a historical purpose, towards which priests and prophets and even politicans had worked, and in which the hope of a nation and a race was embodied. Yet, from the worldly point of view, from the standpoint of a contemporary secular historian, it was not only unimportant, but actually invisible. Here was a Galilean peasant who for thirty years lived a life so obscure as to be unknown even to the disciples who accepted His mission. Then there followed a brief period of public action, which did not lead to any kind of historical achievement but moved swiftly and irresistibly towards its catastrophic end, an end that was foreseen and deliberately accepted.

And out of the heart of this catastrophe there arose something completely new, which even in its success was a deception to the very people and the very race that had staked their hopes on it. For after Pentecost—after the outpouring of the Spirit and the birth of the infant Church—there was an event as unforeseen and inexplicable as the Incarnation itself, the conversion of a Cilician Jew, who turned away from his traditions and from his own people so that he seemed a traitor to his race and his religion. So that ultimately the fulfilment of the hope of Israel meant the rejection of Israel and the creation of a new community which was eventually to become the State religion of the Roman Empire which had been the enemy of Jew and Christian alike.

If you look on all this without faith, from the rationalist point of view, it becomes no easier to understand. On the contrary it becomes even more inexplicable; *credo quia incredibile.*

Now the life of Christ is the life of the Christian and the life of the Church. It is absurd for a Christian who is a weak human vehicle of this world-changing force to expect a quiet life. A Christian is like a red rag to a bull—to the force of evil that seeks to be master of the world and which, in a limited sense, but in a very real sense, is as St. John says the Lord of this world. And not only the individual but the Church as an historic community follows the same pattern and finds its success and failure not where the politician finds them, but where Christ found them.

The Church lives again the life of Christ. It
has its period of obscurity and growth and its
period of manifestation, and this is followed by
the catastrophe of the Cross and the new
birth that springs from failure. And what is
most remarkable is that the enemies of the
Church—the movements that rend and crucify
her—are in a sense her own offspring and derive
their dynamic force from her. Islam, the Protestant Reformation, the Liberal Revolution,
none of them would have existed apart from
Christianity—they are abortive or partial manifestations of the spiritual power which Christianity has brought into history. "I have come to
cast fire on the earth and what will I, but that
it be kindled."

The new situation with which the Church
is faced to-day is of a similar nature. It is
not merely a question of the victory of material-
ism over religion and the triumph of brute force
over right. We are witnessing the rise of new
forms of social life and a new kind of community which aspires to be something more than
the old State. We call it totalitarian in the
bad sense, because it claims to absorb the
individual and admits no rival. But what gives
it its strength is that it aspires to be totalitarian
in a higher sense: to go beyond the practical

utilitarian functions of the individualist State and to embrace the whole of life. It seeks to be, not merely an association for the maintenance of peace and order and the rights of property, but a spiritual community, a fellowship through which the individual attains a higher and more complete life than he can realize by any form of private association.

It is obvious that in practice this new type of community threatens both the freedom of the individual and the autonomy of the Church, since it absorbs the one and competes with the other to a certain extent on its own ground. Nevertheless it is not to be condemned out of hand as evil, since it is an attempt to satisfy a fundamental human need which has been thwarted and repressed by the inhuman forces in modern civilization. Man does not live by bread alone, and he can never feel at home in a community like the nineteenth century individualistic capitalist State, which deliberately confined itself to the lower side of life—which was a broker and a policeman and at need a hangman, but never a king or a priest.

Human nature needs a holy community, and though this need finds satisfaction in a true Christian order, it does not find it in the sect and the chapel which was all the nineteenth century offered to fill the void left by the secular State. Hence, granted the scandal of Christian disunion and the failure of the Church to inspire and mould the subordinate categories of social life, it was inevitable that men should seek satisfaction elsewhere, in a community that was wider than that of the sect and deeper and richer than that of the secular State. If therefore Christians take up a negative attitude to this movement and attack and repudiate it, they may find that they are fighting against God and standing in the path of the march of God through history.

It is true that they cannot abandon themselves uncritically to the wave of emotional idealism that sways the mass. For, though the impulse behind the movement may be good (and even divinely inspired), it is inevitably contaminated with all sorts of impure elements and open to the influence of evil and demonic powers. Hence we must expect that this movement will come into conflict with the Church, even though Christians do not adopt an aggressive attitude. And in that case it is necessary for Christians to bear faithful witness to their Faith at whatever cost.

Nothing is more difficult in practice than this. It is easy to give way to the dominant

tendency to surrender to the spirit of the age
and the spirit of the world by shutting our eyes
to the errors of public opinion and the evils
and injustice of popular action; it is the same
temptation which in the past made religious
men flatter the pride of the great and overlook
the injustice of the powerful. But it is also
easy, and it is a more insidious temptation,
to adopt an attitude of negative hostility to
the spirit of the age and to take refuge in a
narrow and exclusive fanaticism which is
essentially the attitude of the heretic and the
sectarian and which does more to discredit
Christianity and render it ineffective than even
worldliness and time-serving. For the latter are,
so to speak, external to the Church's life,
whereas the former poisons the sources of its
spiritual action and causes it to appear hateful
in the eyes of men of good will.

It is the nature of heresy to sacrifice Catholic
truth and Christian unity by concentrating its
attention on the immediate solution of some
pressing contemporary problem of Christian
thought or action. The heretic goes astray
by attempting to take a short cut, owing to a
natural human impatience at the apparent
slowness and difficulty of the way of pure faith.

But the Church also has to take the difficult

way of the Cross, to incur the penalties and
humiliations of earthly failure without any
compensating hope of temporal success. She is
not an alternative and a rival to the State, and
her teaching does not take the place of political
needs and ideologies; yet she cannot disinterest
herself in the corporate life of the community
and confine her attentions to the individual
soul. The Church is no human society, but she
is the channel by which divine life flows into
human society and her essential task is the
sanctification of humanity as a whole in its
corporate as well as in its individual activities.

Human Society to-day is in a state of rapid
change. The life is going out of the old political
and juridical forms and a new community is
being created whose appearance marks a new
epoch in history. It is not the Church's business
to stop this great social change, and she could
not if she would, but neither can she abdicate
her essential mission, which remains the same
in the new circumstances as of old. The new
social forms offer new opportunities—new
openings for the action of grace.

We are perhaps too much inclined to look
to authority to lay down beforehand a programme of action when the initiative must
come in the first place from the spontaneous

personal reaction of individuals to the circumstances of the moment. It would be of no use
for the Vatican to issue a perfect constitution for
a perfect Catholic State, when Catholics actually
have to deal with the problem of real life where
States are neither perfect nor Catholic and
when even in the natural sphere the statesmen
and organizers of this world do not know what is
going to happen from one day to another.

But whereas this obscurity and incalcul-
ability is inevitably a source of discouragement
to the statesman, whose whole business is to
achieve temporal success, it should be of no
great importance to the Christian who sees the
end of history as dawn and not as night.

When Our Lord spoke of the future He gave
His disciples no optimistic hopes, no visions
of social progress; He described all the things
that we are afraid of to-day and more—wars,
persecutions, disasters and the distress of
nations. But strange to say He used this
forecast of calamity as a motive for hope.
"When you see these things," He said, "look
up and lift up your heads for your redemption
is at hand."

That may seem a strange philosophy of
history, but it is the authentic philosophy of
Christ, and if the prospect of these things

causes us to hang down our heads instead of lifting them up, it shows that there is something wrong with our point of view. I know we are apt to feel this does not apply to us— that it merely refers to the end of the world. But to the Christian the world is always ending, and every historical crisis is, as it were, a rehearsal for the real thing.